I0308878

C-992 CAREER EXAMINATION SERIES

This is your PASSBOOK for...

Senior Accountant

Test Preparation Study Guide
Questions & Answers

NLC®
NATIONAL LEARNING CORPORATION®

COPYRIGHT NOTICE

This book is SOLELY intended for, is sold ONLY to, and its use is RESTRICTED to individual, bona fide applicants or candidates who qualify by virtue of having seriously filed applications for appropriate license, certificate, professional and/or promotional advancement, higher school matriculation, scholarship, or other legitimate requirements of education and/or governmental authorities.

This book is NOT intended for use, class instruction, tutoring, training, duplication, copying, reprinting, excerption, or adaptation, etc., by:

1) Other publishers
2) Proprietors and/or Instructors of “Coaching” and/or Preparatory Courses
3) Personnel and/or Training Divisions of commercial, industrial, and governmental organizations
4) Schools, colleges, or universities and/or their departments and staffs, including teachers and other personnel
5) Testing Agencies or Bureaus
6) Study groups which seek by the purchase of a single volume to copy and/or duplicate and/or adapt this material for use by the group as a whole without having purchased individual volumes for each of the members of the group
7) Et al.

Such persons would be in violation of appropriate Federal and State statutes.

PROVISION OF LICENSING AGREEMENTS – Recognized educational, commercial, industrial, and governmental institutions and organizations, and others legitimately engaged in educational pursuits, including training, testing, and measurement activities, may address request for a licensing agreement to the copyright owners, who will determine whether, and under what conditions, including fees and charges, the materials in this book may be used them. In other words, a licensing facility exists for the legitimate use of the material in this book on other than an individual basis. However, it is asseverated and affirmed here that the material in this book CANNOT be used without the receipt of the express permission of such a licensing agreement from the Publishers. Inquiries re licensing should be addressed to the company, attention rights and permissions department.

All rights reserved, including the right of reproduction in whole or in part, in any form or by any means, electronic or mechanical, including photocopying, recording, or by any information storage and retrieval system, without permission in writing from the Publisher.

Copyright © 2024 by

National Learning Corporation

212 Michael Drive, Syosset, NY 11791
(516) 921-8888 • www.passbooks.com
E-mail: info@passbooks.com

PUBLISHED IN THE UNITED STATES OF AMERICA

COPYRIGHT NOTICE

PASSBOOK® SERIES

THE *PASSBOOK® SERIES* has been created to prepare applicants and candidates for the ultimate academic battlefield – the examination room.

At some time in our lives, each and every one of us may be required to take an examination – for validation, matriculation, admission, qualification, registration, certification, or licensure.

Based on the assumption that every applicant or candidate has met the basic formal educational standards, has taken the required number of courses, and read the necessary texts, the *PASSBOOK® SERIES* furnishes the one special preparation which may assure passing with confidence, instead of failing with insecurity. Examination questions – together with answers – are furnished as the basic vehicle for study so that the mysteries of the examination and its compounding difficulties may be eliminated or diminished by a sure method.

This book is meant to help you pass your examination provided that you qualify and are serious in your objective.

The entire field is reviewed through the huge store of content information which is succinctly presented through a provocative and challenging approach – the question-and-answer method.

A climate of success is established by furnishing the correct answers at the end of each test.

You soon learn to recognize types of questions, forms of questions, and patterns of questioning. You may even begin to anticipate expected outcomes.

You perceive that many questions are repeated or adapted so that you can gain acute insights, which may enable you to score many sure points.

You learn how to confront new questions, or types of questions, and to attack them confidently and work out the correct answers.

You note objectives and emphases, and recognize pitfalls and dangers, so that you may make positive educational adjustments.

Moreover, you are kept fully informed in relation to new concepts, methods, practices, and directions in the field.

You discover that you are actually taking the examination all the time: you are preparing for the examination by "taking" an examination, not by reading extraneous and/or supererogatory textbooks.

In short, this PASSBOOK®, used directedly, should be an important factor in helping you to pass your test.

SENIOR ACCOUNTANT

DUTIES:

An employee in this class performs complex and difficult professional accounting work in maintaining accounting records, preparing reports and assisting in establishing new accounting systems and methods for an accounting section of a large department. In a small department, the incumbent may have overall responsibility for accounting functions including developing and implementing new methods and systems. Supervision is exercised over a number of professional and clerical employees engaged in maintaining financial and accounting records. Work is performed under the general supervision of a Principal Accountant or administrator and is reviewed through periodic audits of records, observation and review of reports, Does related work as required.

EXAMPLES OF DUTIES:

- Supervises and reviews preparation of various monthly journal entries and account reconciliations;
- Reviews department expense statement items and analyzes large fluctuations and budget variances;
- Maintains and reviews operating and capital lease schedule and related accounting records;
- Performs capitalization of fixed assets and projects and maintains records related to depreciation;
- Maintains subsidiary ledgers and prepares corresponding reconciliations;
- Prepares monthly and quarterly sales tax reports;
- Serves as a liaison to independent auditors and departments for providing accounting information;
- Participates in internal audits relating to financial reporting;
- Participates in all required general ledger system upgrades, testing, and documentation;
- Supervises employee input, posting and processing of financial and accounts receivable information into an electronic information system to ensure accuracy and completeness;
- Analyzes information for inclusion in records and reports as required;
- Maintains and distributes information as appropriate;
- Participates in reviewing, compiling and analyzing information for use in collective bargaining negotiations;
- Participates in the preparation and documentation of new policies or standard operating procedures;
- Organizes and participates in meetings and committees as required.

SCOPE OF THE EXAMINATION:

The written test will cover knowledge, skills, and/or abilities in such areas as:

1. General accounting;
2. General auditing;
3. Governmental accounting;
4. Supervision;
5. Understanding and interpreting tabular material; and
6. Preparing written material.

HOW TO TAKE A TEST

I. YOU MUST PASS AN EXAMINATION

A. WHAT EVERY CANDIDATE SHOULD KNOW

Examination applicants often ask us for help in preparing for the written test. What can I study in advance? What kinds of questions will be asked? How will the test be given? How will the papers be graded?

As an applicant for a civil service examination, you may be wondering about some of these things. Our purpose here is to suggest effective methods of advance study and to describe civil service examinations.

Your chances for success on this examination can be increased if you know how to prepare. Those "pre-examination jitters" can be reduced if you know what to expect. You can even experience an adventure in good citizenship if you know why civil service exams are given.

B. WHY ARE CIVIL SERVICE EXAMINATIONS GIVEN?

Civil service examinations are important to you in two ways. As a citizen, you want public jobs filled by employees who know how to do their work. As a job seeker, you want a fair chance to compete for that job on an equal footing with other candidates. The best-known means of accomplishing this two-fold goal is the competitive examination.

Exams are widely publicized throughout the nation. They may be administered for jobs in federal, state, city, municipal, town or village governments or agencies.

Any citizen may apply, with some limitations, such as the age or residence of applicants. Your experience and education may be reviewed to see whether you meet the requirements for the particular examination. When these requirements exist, they are reasonable and applied consistently to all applicants. Thus, a competitive examination may cause you some uneasiness now, but it is your privilege and safeguard.

C. HOW ARE CIVIL SERVICE EXAMS DEVELOPED?

Examinations are carefully written by trained technicians who are specialists in the field known as "psychological measurement," in consultation with recognized authorities in the field of work that the test will cover. These experts recommend the subject matter areas or skills to be tested; only those knowledges or skills important to your success on the job are included. The most reliable books and source materials available are used as references. Together, the experts and technicians judge the difficulty level of the questions.

Test technicians know how to phrase questions so that the problem is clearly stated. Their ethics do not permit "trick" or "catch" questions. Questions may have been tried out on sample groups, or subjected to statistical analysis, to determine their usefulness.

Written tests are often used in combination with performance tests, ratings of training and experience, and oral interviews. All of these measures combine to form the best-known means of finding the right person for the right job.

II. HOW TO PASS THE WRITTEN TEST

A. NATURE OF THE EXAMINATION

To prepare intelligently for civil service examinations, you should know how they differ from school examinations you have taken. In school you were assigned certain definite pages to read or subjects to cover. The examination questions were quite detailed and usually emphasized memory. Civil service exams, on the other hand, try to discover your present ability to perform the duties of a position, plus your potentiality to learn these duties. In other words, a civil service exam attempts to predict how successful you will be. Questions cover such a broad area that they cannot be as minute and detailed as school exam questions.

In the public service similar kinds of work, or positions, are grouped together in one "class." This process is known as *position-classification.* All the positions in a class are paid according to the salary range for that class. One class title covers all of these positions, and they are all tested by the same examination.

B. FOUR BASIC STEPS

1) Study the announcement

How, then, can you know what subjects to study? Our best answer is: "Learn as much as possible about the class of positions for which you've applied." The exam will test the knowledge, skills and abilities needed to do the work.

Your most valuable source of information about the position you want is the official exam announcement. This announcement lists the training and experience qualifications. Check these standards and apply only if you come reasonably close to meeting them.

The brief description of the position in the examination announcement offers some clues to the subjects which will be tested. Think about the job itself. Review the duties in your mind. Can you perform them, or are there some in which you are rusty? Fill in the blank spots in your preparation.

Many jurisdictions preview the written test in the exam announcement by including a section called "Knowledge and Abilities Required," "Scope of the Examination," or some similar heading. Here you will find out specifically what fields will be tested.

2) Review your own background

Once you learn in general what the position is all about, and what you need to know to do the work, ask yourself which subjects you already know fairly well and which need improvement. You may wonder whether to concentrate on improving your strong areas or on building some background in your fields of weakness. When the announcement has specified "some knowledge" or "considerable knowledge," or has used adjectives like "beginning principles of..." or "advanced ... methods," you can get a clue as to the number and difficulty of questions to be asked in any given field. More questions, and hence broader coverage, would be included for those subjects which are more important in the work. Now weigh your strengths and weaknesses against the job requirements and prepare accordingly.

3) Determine the level of the position

Another way to tell how intensively you should prepare is to understand the level of the job for which you are applying. Is it the entering level? In other words, is this the position in which beginners in a field of work are hired? Or is it an intermediate or advanced level? Sometimes this is indicated by such words as "Junior" or "Senior" in the class title. Other jurisdictions use Roman numerals to designate the level – Clerk I, Clerk II, for example. The word "Supervisor" sometimes appears in the title. If the level is not indicated by the title, check the description of duties. Will you be working under very close supervision, or will you have responsibility for independent decisions in this work?

4) Choose appropriate study materials

Now that you know the subjects to be examined and the relative amount of each subject to be covered, you can choose suitable study materials. For beginning level jobs, or even advanced ones, if you have a pronounced weakness in some aspect of your training, read a modern, standard textbook in that field. Be sure it is up to date and has general coverage. Such books are normally available at your library, and the librarian will be glad to help you locate one. For entry-level positions, questions of appropriate difficulty are chosen – neither highly advanced questions, nor those too simple. Such questions require careful thought but not advanced training.

If the position for which you are applying is technical or advanced, you will read more advanced, specialized material. If you are already familiar with the basic principles of your field, elementary textbooks would waste your time. Concentrate on advanced textbooks and technical periodicals. Think through the concepts and review difficult problems in your field.

These are all general sources. You can get more ideas on your own initiative, following these leads. For example, training manuals and publications of the government agency which employs workers in your field can be useful, particularly for technical and professional positions. A letter or visit to the government department involved may result in more specific study suggestions, and certainly will provide you with a more definite idea of the exact nature of the position you are seeking.

III. KINDS OF TESTS

Tests are used for purposes other than measuring knowledge and ability to perform specified duties. For some positions, it is equally important to test ability to make adjustments to new situations or to profit from training. In others, basic mental abilities not dependent on information are essential. Questions which test these things may not appear as pertinent to the duties of the position as those which test for knowledge and information. Yet they are often highly important parts of a fair examination. For very general questions, it is almost impossible to help you direct your study efforts. What we can do is to point out some of the more common of these general abilities needed in public service positions and describe some typical questions.

1) General information

Broad, general information has been found useful for predicting job success in some kinds of work. This is tested in a variety of ways, from vocabulary lists to questions about current events. Basic background in some field of work, such as sociology or economics, may be sampled in a group of questions. Often these are principles which have become familiar to most persons through exposure rather than through formal training. It is difficult to advise you how to study for these questions; being alert to the world around you is our best suggestion.

2) Verbal ability

An example of an ability needed in many positions is verbal or language ability. Verbal ability is, in brief, the ability to use and understand words. Vocabulary and grammar tests are typical measures of this ability. Reading comprehension or paragraph interpretation questions are common in many kinds of civil service tests. You are given a paragraph of written material and asked to find its central meaning.

3) Numerical ability

Number skills can be tested by the familiar arithmetic problem, by checking paired lists of numbers to see which are alike and which are different, or by interpreting charts and graphs. In the latter test, a graph may be printed in the test booklet which you are asked to use as the basis for answering questions.

4) Observation

A popular test for law-enforcement positions is the observation test. A picture is shown to you for several minutes, then taken away. Questions about the picture test your ability to observe both details and larger elements.

5) Following directions

In many positions in the public service, the employee must be able to carry out written instructions dependably and accurately. You may be given a chart with several columns, each column listing a variety of information. The questions require you to carry out directions involving the information given in the chart.

6) Skills and aptitudes

Performance tests effectively measure some manual skills and aptitudes. When the skill is one in which you are trained, such as typing or shorthand, you can practice. These tests are often very much like those given in business school or high school courses. For many of the other skills and aptitudes, however, no short-time preparation can be made. Skills and abilities natural to you or that you have developed throughout your lifetime are being tested.

Many of the general questions just described provide all the data needed to answer the questions and ask you to use your reasoning ability to find the answers. Your best preparation for these tests, as well as for tests of facts and ideas, is to be at your physical and mental best. You, no doubt, have your own methods of getting into an exam-taking mood and keeping "in shape." The next section lists some ideas on this subject.

IV. KINDS OF QUESTIONS

Only rarely is the "essay" question, which you answer in narrative form, used in civil service tests. Civil service tests are usually of the short-answer type. Full instructions for answering these questions will be given to you at the examination. But in case this is your first experience with short-answer questions and separate answer sheets, here is what you need to know:

1) Multiple-choice Questions

Most popular of the short-answer questions is the "multiple choice" or "best answer" question. It can be used, for example, to test for factual knowledge, ability to solve problems or judgment in meeting situations found at work.

A multiple-choice question is normally one of three types—

- It can begin with an incomplete statement followed by several possible endings. You are to find the one ending which *best* completes the statement, although some of the others may not be entirely wrong.
- It can also be a complete statement in the form of a question which is answered by choosing one of the statements listed.

- It can be in the form of a problem – again you select the best answer.

Here is an example of a multiple-choice question with a discussion which should give you some clues as to the method for choosing the right answer:

When an employee has a complaint about his assignment, the action which will *best* help him overcome his difficulty is to

A. discuss his difficulty with his coworkers
B. take the problem to the head of the organization
C. take the problem to the person who gave him the assignment
D. say nothing to anyone about his complaint

In answering this question, you should study each of the choices to find which is best. Consider choice "A" – Certainly an employee may discuss his complaint with fellow employees, but no change or improvement can result, and the complaint remains unresolved. Choice "B" is a poor choice since the head of the organization probably does not know what assignment you have been given, and taking your problem to him is known as "going over the head" of the supervisor. The supervisor, or person who made the assignment, is the person who can clarify it or correct any injustice. Choice "C" is, therefore, correct. To say nothing, as in choice "D," is unwise. Supervisors have and interest in knowing the problems employees are facing, and the employee is seeking a solution to his problem.

2) True/False Questions

The "true/false" or "right/wrong" form of question is sometimes used. Here a complete statement is given. Your job is to decide whether the statement is right or wrong.

SAMPLE: A roaming cell-phone call to a nearby city costs less than a non-roaming call to a distant city.

This statement is wrong, or false, since roaming calls are more expensive.

This is not a complete list of all possible question forms, although most of the others are variations of these common types. You will always get complete directions for answering questions. Be sure you understand *how* to mark your answers – ask questions until you do.

V. RECORDING YOUR ANSWERS

Computer terminals are used more and more today for many different kinds of exams.

For an examination with very few applicants, you may be told to record your answers in the test booklet itself. Separate answer sheets are much more common. If this separate answer sheet is to be scored by machine – and this is often the case – it is highly important that you mark your answers correctly in order to get credit.

An electronic scoring machine is often used in civil service offices because of the speed with which papers can be scored. Machine-scored answer sheets must be marked with a pencil, which will be given to you. This pencil has a high graphite content which responds to the electronic scoring machine. As a matter of fact, stray dots may register as answers, so do not let your pencil rest on the answer sheet while you are pondering the correct answer. Also, if your pencil lead breaks or is otherwise defective, ask for another.

Since the answer sheet will be dropped in a slot in the scoring machine, be careful not to bend the corners or get the paper crumpled.

The answer sheet normally has five vertical columns of numbers, with 30 numbers to a column. These numbers correspond to the question numbers in your test booklet. After each number, going across the page are four or five pairs of dotted lines. These short dotted lines have small letters or numbers above them. The first two pairs may also have a "T" or "F" above the letters. This indicates that the first two pairs only are to be used if the questions are of the true-false type. If the questions are multiple choice, disregard the "T" and "F" and pay attention only to the small letters or numbers.

Answer your questions in the manner of the sample that follows:

32. The largest city in the United States is
    - A. Washington, D.C.
    - B. New York City
    - C. Chicago
    - D. Detroit
    - E. San Francisco

1) Choose the answer you think is best. (New York City is the largest, so "B" is correct.)
2) Find the row of dotted lines numbered the same as the question you are answering. (Find row number 32)
3) Find the pair of dotted lines corresponding to the answer. (Find the pair of lines under the mark "B.")
4) Make a solid black mark between the dotted lines.

VI. BEFORE THE TEST

Common sense will help you find procedures to follow to get ready for an examination. Too many of us, however, overlook these sensible measures. Indeed, nervousness and fatigue have been found to be the most serious reasons why applicants fail to do their best on civil service tests. Here is a list of reminders:

- Begin your preparation early – Don't wait until the last minute to go scurrying around for books and materials or to find out what the position is all about.
- Prepare continuously – An hour a night for a week is better than an all-night cram session. This has been definitely established. What is more, a night a week for a month will return better dividends than crowding your study into a shorter period of time.
- Locate the place of the exam – You have been sent a notice telling you when and where to report for the examination. If the location is in a different town or otherwise unfamiliar to you, it would be well to inquire the best route and learn something about the building.
- Relax the night before the test – Allow your mind to rest. Do not study at all that night. Plan some mild recreation or diversion; then go to bed early and get a good night's sleep.
- Get up early enough to make a leisurely trip to the place for the test – This way unforeseen events, traffic snarls, unfamiliar buildings, etc. will not upset you.
- Dress comfortably – A written test is not a fashion show. You will be known by number and not by name, so wear something comfortable.

- Leave excess paraphernalia at home – Shopping bags and odd bundles will get in your way. You need bring only the items mentioned in the official notice you received; usually everything you need is provided. Do not bring reference books to the exam. They will only confuse those last minutes and be taken away from you when in the test room.
- Arrive somewhat ahead of time – If because of transportation schedules you must get there very early, bring a newspaper or magazine to take your mind off yourself while waiting.
- Locate the examination room – When you have found the proper room, you will be directed to the seat or part of the room where you will sit. Sometimes you are given a sheet of instructions to read while you are waiting. Do not fill out any forms until you are told to do so; just read them and be prepared.
- Relax and prepare to listen to the instructions
- If you have any physical problem that may keep you from doing your best, be sure to tell the test administrator. If you are sick or in poor health, you really cannot do your best on the exam. You can come back and take the test some other time.

VII. AT THE TEST

The day of the test is here and you have the test booklet in your hand. The temptation to get going is very strong. Caution! There is more to success than knowing the right answers. You must know how to identify your papers and understand variations in the type of short-answer question used in this particular examination. Follow these suggestions for maximum results from your efforts:

1) Cooperate with the monitor

The test administrator has a duty to create a situation in which you can be as much at ease as possible. He will give instructions, tell you when to begin, check to see that you are marking your answer sheet correctly, and so on. He is not there to guard you, although he will see that your competitors do not take unfair advantage. He wants to help you do your best.

2) Listen to all instructions

Don't jump the gun! Wait until you understand all directions. In most civil service tests you get more time than you need to answer the questions. So don't be in a hurry. Read each word of instructions until you clearly understand the meaning. Study the examples, listen to all announcements and follow directions. Ask questions if you do not understand what to do.

3) Identify your papers

Civil service exams are usually identified by number only. You will be assigned a number; you must not put your name on your test papers. Be sure to copy your number correctly. Since more than one exam may be given, copy your exact examination title.

4) Plan your time

Unless you are told that a test is a "speed" or "rate of work" test, speed itself is usually not important. Time enough to answer all the questions will be provided, but this does not mean that you have all day. An overall time limit has been set. Divide the total time (in minutes) by the number of questions to determine the approximate time you have for each question.

5) Do not linger over difficult questions

If you come across a difficult question, mark it with a paper clip (useful to have along) and come back to it when you have been through the booklet. One caution if you do this – be sure to skip a number on your answer sheet as well. Check often to be sure that you have not lost your place and that you are marking in the row numbered the same as the question you are answering.

6) Read the questions

Be sure you know what the question asks! Many capable people are unsuccessful because they failed to *read* the questions correctly.

7) Answer all questions

Unless you have been instructed that a penalty will be deducted for incorrect answers, it is better to guess than to omit a question.

8) Speed tests

It is often better NOT to guess on speed tests. It has been found that on timed tests people are tempted to spend the last few seconds before time is called in marking answers at random – without even reading them – in the hope of picking up a few extra points. To discourage this practice, the instructions may warn you that your score will be "corrected" for guessing. That is, a penalty will be applied. The incorrect answers will be deducted from the correct ones, or some other penalty formula will be used.

9) Review your answers

If you finish before time is called, go back to the questions you guessed or omitted to give them further thought. Review other answers if you have time.

10) Return your test materials

If you are ready to leave before others have finished or time is called, take ALL your materials to the monitor and leave quietly. Never take any test material with you. The monitor can discover whose papers are not complete, and taking a test booklet may be grounds for disqualification.

VIII. EXAMINATION TECHNIQUES

1) Read the general instructions carefully. These are usually printed on the first page of the exam booklet. As a rule, these instructions refer to the timing of the examination; the fact that you should not start work until the signal and must stop work at a signal, etc. If there are any *special* instructions, such as a choice of questions to be answered, make sure that you note this instruction carefully.

2) When you are ready to start work on the examination, that is as soon as the signal has been given, read the instructions to each question booklet, underline any key words or phrases, such as *least, best, outline, describe* and the like. In this way you will tend to answer as requested rather than discover on reviewing your paper that you *listed without describing*, that you selected the *worst* choice rather than the *best* choice, etc.

3) If the examination is of the objective or multiple-choice type – that is, each question will also give a series of possible answers: A, B, C or D, and you are called upon to select the best answer and write the letter next to that answer on your answer paper – it is advisable to start answering each question in turn. There may be anywhere from 50 to 100 such questions in the three or four hours allotted and you can see how much time would be taken if you read through all the questions before beginning to answer any. Furthermore, if you come across a question or group of questions which you know would be difficult to answer, it would undoubtedly affect your handling of all the other questions.

4) If the examination is of the essay type and contains but a few questions, it is a moot point as to whether you should read all the questions before starting to answer any one. Of course, if you are given a choice – say five out of seven and the like – then it is essential to read all the questions so you can eliminate the two that are most difficult. If, however, you are asked to answer all the questions, there may be danger in trying to answer the easiest one first because you may find that you will spend too much time on it. The best technique is to answer the first question, then proceed to the second, etc.

5) Time your answers. Before the exam begins, write down the time it started, then add the time allowed for the examination and write down the time it must be completed, then divide the time available somewhat as follows:
   - If 3-1/2 hours are allowed, that would be 210 minutes. If you have 80 objective-type questions, that would be an average of 2-1/2 minutes per question. Allow yourself no more than 2 minutes per question, or a total of 160 minutes, which will permit about 50 minutes to review.
   - If for the time allotment of 210 minutes there are 7 essay questions to answer, that would average about 30 minutes a question. Give yourself only 25 minutes per question so that you have about 35 minutes to review.

6) The most important instruction is to *read each question* and make sure you know what is wanted. The second most important instruction is to *time yourself properly* so that you answer every question. The third most important instruction is to *answer every question.* Guess if you have to but include something for each question. Remember that you will receive no credit for a blank and will probably receive some credit if you write something in answer to an essay question. If you guess a letter – say "B" for a multiple-choice question – you may have guessed right. If you leave a blank as an answer to a multiple-choice question, the examiners may respect your feelings but it will not add a point to your score. Some exams may penalize you for wrong answers, so in such cases *only,* you may not want to guess unless you have some basis for your answer.

7) Suggestions
   a. Objective-type questions
      1. Examine the question booklet for proper sequence of pages and questions
      2. Read all instructions carefully
      3. Skip any question which seems too difficult; return to it after all other questions have been answered
      4. Apportion your time properly; do not spend too much time on any single question or group of questions

5. Note and underline key words – *all, most, fewest, least, best, worst, same, opposite,* etc.
6. Pay particular attention to negatives
7. Note unusual option, e.g., unduly long, short, complex, different or similar in content to the body of the question
8. Observe the use of "hedging" words – *probably, may, most likely,* etc.
9. Make sure that your answer is put next to the same number as the question
10. Do not second-guess unless you have good reason to believe the second answer is definitely more correct
11. Cross out original answer if you decide another answer is more accurate; do not erase until you are ready to hand your paper in
12. Answer all questions; guess unless instructed otherwise
13. Leave time for review

b. Essay questions
1. Read each question carefully
2. Determine exactly what is wanted. Underline key words or phrases.
3. Decide on outline or paragraph answer
4. Include many different points and elements unless asked to develop any one or two points or elements
5. Show impartiality by giving pros and cons unless directed to select one side only
6. Make and write down any assumptions you find necessary to answer the questions
7. Watch your English, grammar, punctuation and choice of words
8. Time your answers; don't crowd material

8) Answering the essay question

Most essay questions can be answered by framing the specific response around several key words or ideas. Here are a few such key words or ideas:

M's: manpower, materials, methods, money, management
P's: purpose, program, policy, plan, procedure, practice, problems, pitfalls, personnel, public relations

a. Six basic steps in handling problems:
1. Preliminary plan and background development
2. Collect information, data and facts
3. Analyze and interpret information, data and facts
4. Analyze and develop solutions as well as make recommendations
5. Prepare report and sell recommendations
6. Install recommendations and follow up effectiveness

b. Pitfalls to avoid
1. *Taking things for granted* – A statement of the situation does not necessarily imply that each of the elements is necessarily true; for example, a complaint may be invalid and biased so that all that can be taken for granted is that a complaint has been registered

2. *Considering only one side of a situation* – Wherever possible, indicate several alternatives and then point out the reasons you selected the best one
3. *Failing to indicate follow up* – Whenever your answer indicates action on your part, make certain that you will take proper follow-up action to see how successful your recommendations, procedures or actions turn out to be
4. *Taking too long in answering any single question* – Remember to time your answers properly

IX. AFTER THE TEST

Scoring procedures differ in detail among civil service jurisdictions although the general principles are the same. Whether the papers are hand-scored or graded by machine we have described, they are nearly always graded by number. That is, the person who marks the paper knows only the number – never the name – of the applicant. Not until all the papers have been graded will they be matched with names. If other tests, such as training and experience or oral interview ratings have been given, scores will be combined. Different parts of the examination usually have different weights. For example, the written test might count 60 percent of the final grade, and a rating of training and experience 40 percent. In many jurisdictions, veterans will have a certain number of points added to their grades.

After the final grade has been determined, the names are placed in grade order and an eligible list is established. There are various methods for resolving ties between those who get the same final grade – probably the most common is to place first the name of the person whose application was received first. Job offers are made from the eligible list in the order the names appear on it. You will be notified of your grade and your rank as soon as all these computations have been made. This will be done as rapidly as possible.

People who are found to meet the requirements in the announcement are called "eligibles." Their names are put on a list of eligible candidates. An eligible's chances of getting a job depend on how high he stands on this list and how fast agencies are filling jobs from the list.

When a job is to be filled from a list of eligibles, the agency asks for the names of people on the list of eligibles for that job. When the civil service commission receives this request, it sends to the agency the names of the three people highest on this list. Or, if the job to be filled has specialized requirements, the office sends the agency the names of the top three persons who meet these requirements from the general list.

The appointing officer makes a choice from among the three people whose names were sent to him. If the selected person accepts the appointment, the names of the others are put back on the list to be considered for future openings.

That is the rule in hiring from all kinds of eligible lists, whether they are for typist, carpenter, chemist, or something else. For every vacancy, the appointing officer has his choice of any one of the top three eligibles on the list. This explains why the person whose name is on top of the list sometimes does not get an appointment when some of the persons lower on the list do. If the appointing officer chooses the second or third eligible, the No. 1 eligible does not get a job at once, but stays on the list until he is appointed or the list is terminated.

X. HOW TO PASS THE INTERVIEW TEST

The examination for which you applied requires an oral interview test. You have already taken the written test and you are now being called for the interview test – the final part of the formal examination.

You may think that it is not possible to prepare for an interview test and that there are no procedures to follow during an interview. Our purpose is to point out some things you can do in advance that will help you and some good rules to follow and pitfalls to avoid while you are being interviewed.

What is an interview supposed to test?

The written examination is designed to test the technical knowledge and competence of the candidate; the oral is designed to evaluate intangible qualities, not readily measured otherwise, and to establish a list showing the relative fitness of each candidate – as measured against his competitors – for the position sought. Scoring is not on the basis of "right" and "wrong," but on a sliding scale of values ranging from "not passable" to "outstanding." As a matter of fact, it is possible to achieve a relatively low score without a single "incorrect" answer because of evident weakness in the qualities being measured.

Occasionally, an examination may consist entirely of an oral test – either an individual or a group oral. In such cases, information is sought concerning the technical knowledges and abilities of the candidate, since there has been no written examination for this purpose. More commonly, however, an oral test is used to supplement a written examination.

Who conducts interviews?

The composition of oral boards varies among different jurisdictions. In nearly all, a representative of the personnel department serves as chairman. One of the members of the board may be a representative of the department in which the candidate would work. In some cases, "outside experts" are used, and, frequently, a businessman or some other representative of the general public is asked to serve. Labor and management or other special groups may be represented. The aim is to secure the services of experts in the appropriate field.

However the board is composed, it is a good idea (and not at all improper or unethical) to ascertain in advance of the interview who the members are and what groups they represent. When you are introduced to them, you will have some idea of their backgrounds and interests, and at least you will not stutter and stammer over their names.

What should be done before the interview?

While knowledge about the board members is useful and takes some of the surprise element out of the interview, there is other preparation which is more substantive. It *is* possible to prepare for an oral interview – in several ways:

1) Keep a copy of your application and review it carefully before the interview

This may be the only document before the oral board, and the starting point of the interview. Know what education and experience you have listed there, and the sequence and dates of all of it. Sometimes the board will ask you to review the highlights of your experience for them; you should not have to hem and haw doing it.

2) Study the class specification and the examination announcement

Usually, the oral board has one or both of these to guide them. The qualities, characteristics or knowledges required by the position sought are stated in these documents. They offer valuable clues as to the nature of the oral interview. For example, if the job involves supervisory responsibilities, the announcement will usually indicate that knowledge of modern supervisory methods and the qualifications of the candidate as a supervisor will be tested. If so, you can expect such questions, frequently in the form of a hypothetical situation which you are expected to solve. NEVER go into an oral without knowledge of the duties and responsibilities of the job you seek.

3) Think through each qualification required

Try to visualize the kind of questions you would ask if you were a board member. How well could you answer them? Try especially to appraise your own knowledge and background in each area, *measured against the job sought*, and identify any areas in which you are weak. Be critical and realistic – do not flatter yourself.

4) Do some general reading in areas in which you feel you may be weak

For example, if the job involves supervision and your past experience has NOT, some general reading in supervisory methods and practices, particularly in the field of human relations, might be useful. Do NOT study agency procedures or detailed manuals. The oral board will be testing your understanding and capacity, not your memory.

5) Get a good night's sleep and watch your general health and mental attitude

You will want a clear head at the interview. Take care of a cold or any other minor ailment, and of course, no hangovers.

What should be done on the day of the interview?

Now comes the day of the interview itself. Give yourself plenty of time to get there. Plan to arrive somewhat ahead of the scheduled time, particularly if your appointment is in the fore part of the day. If a previous candidate fails to appear, the board might be ready for you a bit early. By early afternoon an oral board is almost invariably behind schedule if there are many candidates, and you may have to wait. Take along a book or magazine to read, or your application to review, but leave any extraneous material in the waiting room when you go in for your interview. In any event, relax and compose yourself.

The matter of dress is important. The board is forming impressions about you – from your experience, your manners, your attitude, and your appearance. Give your personal appearance careful attention. Dress your best, but not your flashiest. Choose conservative, appropriate clothing, and be sure it is immaculate. This is a business interview, and your appearance should indicate that you regard it as such. Besides, being well groomed and properly dressed will help boost your confidence.

Sooner or later, someone will call your name and escort you into the interview room. *This is it.* From here on you are on your own. It is too late for any more preparation. But remember, you asked for this opportunity to prove your fitness, and you are here because your request was granted.

What happens when you go in?

The usual sequence of events will be as follows: The clerk (who is often the board stenographer) will introduce you to the chairman of the oral board, who will introduce you to the other members of the board. Acknowledge the introductions before you sit down. Do not be surprised if you find a microphone facing you or a stenotypist sitting by. Oral interviews are usually recorded in the event of an appeal or other review.

Usually the chairman of the board will open the interview by reviewing the highlights of your education and work experience from your application – primarily for the benefit of the other members of the board, as well as to get the material into the record. Do not interrupt or comment unless there is an error or significant misinterpretation; if that is the case, do not hesitate. But do not quibble about insignificant matters. Also, he will usually ask you some question about your education, experience or your present job – partly to get you to start talking and to establish the interviewing "rapport." He may start the actual questioning, or turn it over to one of the other members. Frequently, each member undertakes the questioning on a particular area, one in which he is perhaps most competent, so you can expect each member to participate in the examination. Because time is limited, you may also expect some rather abrupt switches in the direction the questioning takes, so do not be upset by it. Normally, a board member will not pursue a single line of questioning unless he discovers a particular strength or weakness.

After each member has participated, the chairman will usually ask whether any member has any further questions, then will ask you if you have anything you wish to add. Unless you are expecting this question, it may floor you. Worse, it may start you off on an extended, extemporaneous speech. The board is not usually seeking more information. The question is principally to offer you a last opportunity to present further qualifications or to indicate that you have nothing to add. So, if you feel that a significant qualification or characteristic has been overlooked, it is proper to point it out in a sentence or so. Do not compliment the board on the thoroughness of their examination – they have been sketchy, and you know it. If you wish, merely say, "No thank you, I have nothing further to add." This is a point where you can "talk yourself out" of a good impression or fail to present an important bit of information. Remember, *you close the interview yourself.*

The chairman will then say, "That is all, Mr. ______, thank you." Do not be startled; the interview is over, and quicker than you think. Thank him, gather your belongings and take your leave. Save your sigh of relief for the other side of the door.

How to put your best foot forward

Throughout this entire process, you may feel that the board individually and collectively is trying to pierce your defenses, seek out your hidden weaknesses and embarrass and confuse you. Actually, this is not true. They are obliged to make an appraisal of your qualifications for the job you are seeking, and they want to see you in your best light. Remember, they must interview all candidates and a non-cooperative candidate may become a failure in spite of their best efforts to bring out his qualifications. Here are 15 suggestions that will help you:

1) Be natural – Keep your attitude confident, not cocky

If you are not confident that you can do the job, do not expect the board to be. Do not apologize for your weaknesses, try to bring out your strong points. The board is interested in a positive, not negative, presentation. Cockiness will antagonize any board member and make him wonder if you are covering up a weakness by a false show of strength.

2) Get comfortable, but don't lounge or sprawl

Sit erectly but not stiffly. A careless posture may lead the board to conclude that you are careless in other things, or at least that you are not impressed by the importance of the occasion. Either conclusion is natural, even if incorrect. Do not fuss with your clothing, a pencil or an ashtray. Your hands may occasionally be useful to emphasize a point; do not let them become a point of distraction.

3) Do not wisecrack or make small talk

This is a serious situation, and your attitude should show that you consider it as such. Further, the time of the board is limited – they do not want to waste it, and neither should you.

4) Do not exaggerate your experience or abilities

In the first place, from information in the application or other interviews and sources, the board may know more about you than you think. Secondly, you probably will not get away with it. An experienced board is rather adept at spotting such a situation, so do not take the chance.

5) If you know a board member, do not make a point of it, yet do not hide it

Certainly you are not fooling him, and probably not the other members of the board. Do not try to take advantage of your acquaintanceship – it will probably do you little good.

6) Do not dominate the interview

Let the board do that. They will give you the clues – do not assume that you have to do all the talking. Realize that the board has a number of questions to ask you, and do not try to take up all the interview time by showing off your extensive knowledge of the answer to the first one.

7) Be attentive

You only have 20 minutes or so, and you should keep your attention at its sharpest throughout. When a member is addressing a problem or question to you, give him your undivided attention. Address your reply principally to him, but do not exclude the other board members.

8) Do not interrupt

A board member may be stating a problem for you to analyze. He will ask you a question when the time comes. Let him state the problem, and wait for the question.

9) Make sure you understand the question

Do not try to answer until you are sure what the question is. If it is not clear, restate it in your own words or ask the board member to clarify it for you. However, do not haggle about minor elements.

10) Reply promptly but not hastily

A common entry on oral board rating sheets is "candidate responded readily," or "candidate hesitated in replies." Respond as promptly and quickly as you can, but do not jump to a hasty, ill-considered answer.

11) Do not be peremptory in your answers

A brief answer is proper – but do not fire your answer back. That is a losing game from your point of view. The board member can probably ask questions much faster than you can answer them.

12) Do not try to create the answer you think the board member wants

He is interested in what kind of mind you have and how it works – not in playing games. Furthermore, he can usually spot this practice and will actually grade you down on it.

13) Do not switch sides in your reply merely to agree with a board member

Frequently, a member will take a contrary position merely to draw you out and to see if you are willing and able to defend your point of view. Do not start a debate, yet do not surrender a good position. If a position is worth taking, it is worth defending.

14) Do not be afraid to admit an error in judgment if you are shown to be wrong

The board knows that you are forced to reply without any opportunity for careful consideration. Your answer may be demonstrably wrong. If so, admit it and get on with the interview.

15) Do not dwell at length on your present job

The opening question may relate to your present assignment. Answer the question but do not go into an extended discussion. You are being examined for a *new* job, not your present one. As a matter of fact, try to phrase ALL your answers in terms of the job for which you are being examined.

Basis of Rating

Probably you will forget most of these "do's" and "don'ts" when you walk into the oral interview room. Even remembering them all will not ensure you a passing grade. Perhaps you did not have the qualifications in the first place. But remembering them will help you to put your best foot forward, without treading on the toes of the board members.

Rumor and popular opinion to the contrary notwithstanding, an oral board wants you to make the best appearance possible. They know you are under pressure – but they also want to see how you respond to it as a guide to what your reaction would be under the pressures of the job you seek. They will be influenced by the degree of poise you display, the personal traits you show and the manner in which you respond.

ABOUT THIS BOOK

This book contains tests divided into Examination Sections. Go through each test, answering every question in the margin. We have also attached a sample answer sheet at the back of the book that can be removed and used. At the end of each test look at the answer key and check your answers. On the ones you got wrong, look at the right answer choice and learn. Do not fill in the answers first. Do not memorize the questions and answers, but understand the answer and principles involved. On your test, the questions will likely be different from the samples. Questions are changed and new ones added. If you understand these past questions you should have success with any changes that arise. Tests may consist of several types of questions. We have additional books on each subject should more study be advisable or necessary for you. Finally, the more you study, the better prepared you will be. This book is intended to be the last thing you study before you walk into the examination room. Prior study of relevant texts is also recommended. NLC publishes some of these in our Fundamental Series. Knowledge and good sense are important factors in passing your exam. Good luck also helps. So now study this Passbook, absorb the material contained within and take that knowledge into the examination. Then do your best to pass that exam.

EXAMINATION SECTION

EXAMINATION SECTION
TEST 1

DIRECTIONS: Each question or incomplete statement is followed by several suggested answers or completions.Select the one that BEST answers the question or completes the statement. *PRINT THE LETTER OF THE CORRECT ANSWER IN THE SPACE AT THE RIGHT.*

1. With regard to the requirement of the auditing standard that sufficient and competent evidential matter be obtained, the term competent PRIMARILY refers to the evidence. 1._____
   - A. consistency
   - B. relevance
   - C. measurability
   - D. dependability

2. Audit working papers should NOT 2._____
   - A. include any client-prepared papers or documents other than those prepared by the auditor
   - B. be kept by the auditor after review and completion of the audit except for items required for the income tax return
   - C. be submitted to the client to support the financial statements and to provide evidence of the audit work performed
   - D. by themselves be expected to provide sufficient support for the auditor's operation

3. Mr. Jason Stone operates a small drugstore as an individual proprietor. During the past year, his books were not properly kept. He asks you, as a CPA, to give him some advice concerning the earnings of his business during the calendar year 2011. A review of his bank accounts and a diary of financial data reveal the information presented below: 3._____

   Deposits made during 2018 per bank statements totaled $226,000. Deposits include investments made by Mr. Shea as well as a loan he obtained from the bank for $25,000.
   Disbursements during 2018 per bank statement totaled $185,000. Included are personal withdrawals of $15,000 and payments on debt of $10,000.
   Net equity of Jason Stone at January 1, 2018 was determined to be $45,000.
   Net equity of Jason Stone at December 31, 2018 was determined to be $75,000.
   During 2018, funds invested by Jason Stone in the business amounted to $6,500.

   Based upon the *net worth* method, net income for the year ended December, 2018 was
   - A. $35,000
   - B. $38,500
   - C. $40,000
   - D. $42,000

4. Because of past association, a senior accountant is convinced of the competence and honesty of those who prepared the financial information which he is auditing. He consequently concludes that certain verification procedures are unnecessary. This conclusion by the senior accountant is ill-advised for the proper performance of his present audit MAINLY because the 4._____
   - A. members of the staff often lack the specialized skills and training without which verification in an audit cannot proceed
   - B. verification procedures depend upon the materiality of the subject matter under examination and not upon the personal characteristics of the individuals involved
   - C. nature of opinion expressed in the report issued by the senior accountant, at the end of his audit, is grounded on personal considerations
   - D. quality of the senior accountant's independence and his objective examination of the information under review is impaired

5. Of the following statement ratios, the one that represents *a growth ratio is* 5.____
   A. working capital ratio
   B. acid-test ratio
   C. long-term debt to total capitalization
   D. dollar earnings per share

Questions-6-8.

DIRECTIONS: Questions 6 through 8 are to be answered on the basis of the information given below.

During the course of an examinations of the financial statements of a wholesale establishment, the following facts were revealed for the year ended December 3, 2018:

I. Although merchandise: inventory costing $3,000 was on hand and.was-included in the inventory count on December 31, 2018, title had passed and it was billed to the customer on December 31, 2018 at a sale price of $4,500.
II. Merchandise had been billed to the customer on December 31, 2018 in the amount of $5,200 but had not been shipped to him. This merchandise which cost $3,500, was not included in the inventory at the end of the year. The goods were shipped and title passed on January 15, 2019.
III. Merchandise costing $6,000 was recorded as a purchase on December 31, 2018 but was Not included in the inventory at that date.
IV. Merchandise costing $5,000 was received on January 3, 2019, but was recorded on the books as of December 31,2018, and included in inventory as of December 31, 2018. The goods were shipped on December 30, 2018 by the vendor F.O.B. shipping point.
V. An examination of receiving records indicated that merchandise costing $7,000 was received on December 31, 2018. It was included in inventory as of that date but not recorded as a purchase.

6. Adjustments to correct the inventory figure will reflect a net adjustment so as to 6.____
   A. reduce it by $6,500
   B. increase it by $6,500
   C. reduce it by $8,000
   D. increase it by $8,000

7. Adjustments to correct the sales figure will result in a net adjustment to sales of a (n) 7.____
   A. increase by $5,200
   B. decrease by $5,200
   C. increase by $6,300
   D. decrease by $6,300

8. The net adjustment to purchases for the period ending December 31, 2018 will result in a(n) 8.____
   A. increase of $4,000
   B. decrease of $7,000
   C. increase of $7,000
   D. decrease of $4,000

Questions 9-10.

DIRECTIONS: Questions 9 and 10 are to be answered on the basis of the information given below.

A company worth $500,000 of common capital stock, par value $100 per share with retained earnings of $100,000, decides to change its capitalization from a par to a no-par basis. It, therefore, called in its 5,000 shares of par value stock and issued in place thereof 10,000 shares of no-par value stock.

9. The balance in the capital stock account after the change is 9.______
   A. $1,000,000 B. $500,000
   C. $,400,000 D. $200,000

10. The balance in the retained earnings account after the change is 10.______
   A. $90,000 B. $100,000 C. $125,000 D. $250,000

11. Among the assets on the December 31, 2018 balance sheet of the Wolf Corporation was the following: 11.______
   Investment in Sheep Company
   1,000 shares @ $90 bought January 1, 2018 $90,000
   The net worth section of the balance sheet of the Sheep Company on the same date was as follows:

NET WORTH		
Capital Stock, 1,000 shares		$100,000
Deficit January 1, 2018	$20,000	
Less Operating Profit 2018	15,000	
Deficit December 31, 2018		5,000
Total Net worth		$ 95,000

   The net debit or credit to Consolidated Surplus arising from consolidation of the Sheep Company with the parent Wolf Corporation is
   A. $3,000 credit B. $5,000 credit
   C. $7,000 debit D. $10,000 credit

Questions 12-15.

DIRECTIONS: Questions 12 through 15 are to be answered on the basis of the Trial Balances and the Notes below.

CLIMAX CORPORATION - Trial Balances (000 Omitted)

	December 31, 2018		December 31, 2017	
	Debit	Credit	Debit	Credit
Cash	$ 178		$ 84	
Accounts Receivable	300		240	
Allowance for Bad Debts		$ 13		$ 10
Merchandise Inventory	370		400	
Building & Equipment	420		360	
Allowance for Depreciation		180		190
Accounts Payable		220		210
Mortgage Bonds		300		300
Unamortized Bond Discount	18			21
Capital Stock		357		270
Retained Earnings		125		90
Net Sales		$4,200		$4,000
Cost of Goods Sold	$2,300		$2,100	
Salaries & Wages	1,500		1,400	
Heat & Utilities	110		100	
Depreciation	20		20	
Taxes & Insurance	10		10	
Interest	16		15	
Bad Debts	20		20	
Losso on Equipment Sales (Note 1)	6		—	
Dividends Paid (Note 2)	127		300	
	$5,395	$5,395	$5,070	$5,070

NOTES: (1) In 2018 equipment costing $40,000 and having a net bookvalue of $10,000 was sold for $4,000.
(2) Dividends paid in 2018 include a stock dividend of $27,000.

12. The net change in working capital from 2017 to 2018 is 12.______
A. $111,000 B. $130,000 C. $260,000 D. $333,000

13. The amount of funds provided from net income for the year ended December 31, 2018 is 13.______
A. $214,000 B. $244,000 C. $254,000 D. $284,000

14. The amount of funds applied to dividends during the year 2018 is 14.______
A. $100,000 B. $125,000 C. $175,000 D. $202,350

15. The amount of funds applied to building and equipment during the year 2018 is 15.______
A. $100,000 B. $70,000 C. $50,000 D. $30,000

Questions 16-17.

DIRECTIONS: Questions 16 and 17 are to be answered on the basis of the information given below.

The Natural Sales Company issues gift certificates in denominations of $5, $10 and $25. They are redeemable in merchandise having a markup of 30% of Selling Price.

During December, $35,000 of gift certificates was sold and $20,000 was redeemed. It is estimated that 5% of the certificates issued will never be redeemed.

16. The PROPER entry to reflect the current liability with respect to these certificates is 16.______
A. $13,250 B. $14,250 C. $15,250 D. $16,250

17. The cost of the merchandise issued to meet the redeemed certificates is 17.______
A. $11,000 B. $13,000 C. $14,000 D. $17,000

Questions 18-19.

DIRECTIONS: Questions 18 and 19 are to be answered on the basis of the information given below.

Arthur Evans commenced business in 2017 but did not maintain a complete set of proper records. He relied on the bank statements in order to compute his income. All his receipts Are deposited, and all his expenditures are made by check.

His bank statements and other records reflected the following:

Bank balance per bank 12/31/2017	$ 14,735
Bank balance per bank 12/31/2018	18,380
Deposits for 2018 per bank statement	209,450
Deposits in transit 12/31/2017	3,590
Deposits in transit 12/31/2018	4,150

Checks returned with the January 2018 bank statement showed a total of $4,770 checks issued in 2018.

2018 checks not returned by the bank at December 31, 2018 amounted to $5,150.

$6,430 of checks were issued in 2018 in payment of purchases made in 2017.

$9,425 of deposits was made by Mr. Evans in 2018 representing 2017 sales.

Unpaid bills for 2018 amounted to $2,150 on December 31, 2018.

Accounts Receivable for 2018 on December 31, 2018 were $10,930.
Merchandise inventory figures on the following dates were:

December 31, 2017	$13,000
December 31, 2018	17,580

On July 1, 2018, machinery costing $8,000 was purchased. The estimated life was 5 years with a salvage value of $500.

18. The balance of the cash in the bank according to the books on December 31, 2018 was 18.______
A. $18,380 B. $17,380 C. $16,380 D. $15,380

19. The Sales Revenue for 2018 was 19.______
A. $211,515 B. $209,515 C. $208,515 D. $207,515

Questions 20-21.

DIRECTIONS: Questions 20 and 21 are to be answered on the basis of the information given below.

In the examination of an imprest petty cash fund of $600, you were presented with the following fund composition shown below. The date of examining the petty cash fund was the balance sheet date.

Currency - bills	$310.00
Cash - coins	3.15
Postage stamps	50.00
Sales returns memos for cash refunded to customers	15.50
Check of one employee dated one month in advance	75.00
Vouchers for miscellaneous office expenses	100.85
Sales slip of an employee who purchased company merchandise; the money in payment was taken from the fund, entered as cash sale, and the sales slip inserted in the fund	45.50

20. The corrected balance of petty cash for balance sheet purposes is 20.______
A. $313.15 B. $319.32 C. $347.53 D. $409.27

21. A correcting journal entry to establish the correct fund balance would increase expenses by 21.______
A. $100.85 B. $212.31 C. $28.28 D. $139.50

22. The PRIMARY objective of an audit, as generally understood in accounting practice, is to 22.______
A. assert a series of claims for management as to the financial condition of the company
B. establish the reliability or unreliability as to the financial statements and supporting accounting records of the company
C. install special procedures involved in the periodic closing of the accounts prior to the preparation of financial statements of the company
D. summarize accounts and financial transactions to determine the costs of processes or units of production for the company

Questions 23-25.

DIRECTIONS: Questions 23 through 25 are to be answered on the basis of the information given below.

The following data related to the business operations for the calendar years 2016, 2017, and 2018 of the Wholly Corporation.

	2016	2017	2018
Net income per books	$170,000	$190,000	$140,000
Dividends	15,000	20,000	10,000
Purchases made in year 2017 recorded as purchased in 2018 but recorded in inventory in 2017		25,000	
Inventory value December 31, 2018 underestimated			5,000
Depreciation omitted -			
applicable to 2016	3,000		
applicable to 2017		4,500	
applicable to 2018			6,000
Overstatement of prepaid advertising as of January 1, 2017		1,500	
Salaries - earned during 2016 paid during 2017 - no accruals	18,000		
Payroll taxes on salarie	1,440		

23. The net profit for 2016 after adjusting for the facts given above is 23.____
    A. $146,060 B. $150,050 C. $164,200 D. $192,835

24. The net profit for 2017 after adjusting for facts given 24.____
    A. $152,400 B. $165,700 C. $173,145 D. $181,440

25. If the balance of the retained earnings account was $265,000 on January1, 2016, the balance of the retainedearnings account on December 31, 2018 after corrections is 25.____
    A. $711,500 B. $525,000 C. $424,360 D. $307,420

Questions 26-30.

DIRECTIONS: Each question numbered 26 through 30 consists of a description of a transaction that indicates a two fold change on the balance sheet. Each of these transactions may be classified under one of the following categories. Examine each question carefully. In the correspondingly numbered space at the right, mark the appropriate space for the letter preceding the category below which BEST represents the charges that should be made on the balance sheet, as of December 31, 2017.

A. Current Assets are *overstated* and Retained Earnings are *overstated*
B. Current Assets are *understated* and Retained Earnings are *understated*
C. Current Liabilities are *overstated* and Retained Earnings are *overstated*
D. Current Liabilities are *understated* and Retained Earnings are *overstated*

26. Goods shipped on consignment out were not included in the final inventory although the entries were properly madefor such consignments. 26.____

27. A number of cash sales made subsequent to the balance sheet date were recorded as sales in the prior periodbefore the balance sheet date. The merchandise was included in inventories. 27.____

28. A cash dividend declared December 21, 2017, payable on January 15, 2018 to stockholders of record as of December 28, 2017, had not been recorded as of December 31, 2017. 28.____

29. The provision for the allowance for doubtful accounts receivable for the current period that should have been made had not been recorded. 29.____

30. Merchandise received by December 31, 2017, and properly included in inventory on that date, was not entered as a purchase until January 2018. 30.____

Questions 31-33.

DIRECTIONS: Questions 31 through 33 are to be answered on the basis of the information given below.

Ten men work as a group on a particular manufacturing operation. When the weekly production of the group exceeds a standard number of pieces per hour, each man in the group is paid a bonus for the excess production; the bonus is in addition to his wages at the hourly rate. The amount of the bonus is computed by first determining the percentage by which the groups production exceeds the standard. One-half of this percentage is then applied to a wage rate of $1.25 to determine an hourly bonus rate. Each man in the group is paid, as a bonus, the bonus rate applied to his total hours worked during the week. The standard rate of production before a bonus can be earned is two hundred pieces per hour.

The production record for a given week was: Hours Worked Production

Days	Hours worked	Production
Monday	72	17,680
Tuesday	72	17,348
Wednesday	72	18,800
Thuresday	72	18,560
Friday	71.5	17,888
Saturday	40	9,600
	399.5	99,076

31. The rate of the bonus for the week is_____ %. 31.____
A. 24 B. 20 C. 18 D. 12

32. The bonus paid to the ten-man group for the week is 32.____
A. $59.93 B. $69.39 C. $95.00 D. $225.00

33. The total wages of one employee who worked 40 hours at a base rate of $1.00 per hour are 33.____
A. $46 B. $50 C. $54 D. $58

34. A junior accountant reported to his senior that he had performed the operations listed below. 34.____
Which one of the following statements about these operations CORRECTLY describes the operation?
A. Vouchered the amount of petty cash
B. Vouchered.the receivables ledger accounts with the sales register
C. Analyzed the fixed assets account
D. Checked all entries in the general journal to original evidence

35. Sales during July 2018 for the Major Company were $267,500, of which $170,000 was on account. The sales figure presented to you includes the total sales tax charged to retail customers (assume a sales tax rate of 7%). 35.____
The sales tax liability that should be shown at the end of July 2018 is
A. $8,300 B. $9,400
C. $17,500 D. $18,750

Questions 36-37.

DIRECTIONS: Questions 36 and 37 are to be answered on the basis of the information given below.

During the audit of records of the Short Corporation for the year ended December 31, 2018, the auditor was presented with the following information:

The finished goods inventory consisted of 22,000 units carried at a cost of $17,600 at December 31, 2018. The finished goods inventory at the beginning of the year (January 1, 2018) consisted of 24,000 units, priced at a cost of $16,800. During the year, 4,000 units were manufactured at a cost of$3,600 and 6,000 units were sold.

36. To PROPERLY reflect the cost of the finished goods inventory at December 31, 2018, if the FIFO method was used, assuming there was no work-in-process inventory, would require an adjustment of 36.____
A. $1,400 credit B. $1,400 debit C.$1,600 credit D. $1,600 debit

37. To PROPERLY reflect the cost of the finished goods inventory at December 31, 2018 if the LIFO method was used, assuming there was no work-in-process Inventory, would require an adjustment of 37.____
A. $2,200 debit B. $2,200 credit C. $4,200 credit D. $4,200 debit

38. Within the general field of auditing, there are internal auditors and independent auditors who differ significantly one from the other in that the latter group: 38.____

A. is responsible for a more complete, detailed examination of accounting data
B. conduct standard audits established by custom and usage for a particular trade or industry
C. direct their investigations primarily to matters of fraud and criminal'misrepresentation
D. issue reports for the benefit of other interests, such as shareholders and creditors

39. Moreland Corporation sells merchandise at a gross profit of 25% of sales. Fire on the premises of this Corporation on July 16, 2018 resulted in the destruction of the merchandise. The Corporation's merchandise is insured against fire by a $150,000 insurance policy with an 80% co-insurance clause. The Corporation's records show the following: 39._____

Sales -- January 1, 2018 to July 16, 2018	$400,000
Inventory -- January 1, 2018	$ 65,000
Purchases -- January 1, 2018 to July16, 2018	$460,000
Merchandise salvaged	$ 25,000

The amount of inventory destroyed by fire is

A. $150,000 B. $200,000 C. $225,000 D. $300,000

40. Below are the totals of the cash receipts and disbursement books of the Small Corporation for the calendar year 2018 40._____

Receipts $392,369.72
Disbursements $331,477.87

The bank balance on January 1, 2018 was $38,610.21. The bank balance on December 31, 2018 was $101,918.34. No checks were outstanding on January 1, 2018. Checks out standing on December 31, 2018 amounted to $5,416.28. Undeposited checks on hand December 31, 2018 were $3,000. which are included in the December cash receipts. Bank deposits for the year total $387,643.72.

The total SHORTAGE in cash is

A. $1,726 B. $2,416.28 C. $3,000 D. $3,452

41. A state corporation, all of whose business is done within the city, showed the following for 2018: 41._____

Entire net income	$ 1,000
Salaries to Officers deducted in determining entire net income	$ 40,000
Average capital	$ 450,000

The corporation's city business tax payable (assuming a 7% rate on income and a .001 rate on capital) is

A. $546 B. $450 C. $70 D. $25

42. Sales revenue serves as the basis for determining taxes. 42._____

A. estate B. excise C. payroll D. property.

43. ABC Corporation operates in the city and would be subjected to the following taxes: 43._____

I. Federal Corporation Income Tax – Surtax 26% and Normal Tax 22%
II. State Franchise Tax - 72%

If income before taxes for 2018 was $370,000 per the federal tax return (after establishing estimate), assuming the rates as noted above, the tax liabilities that should be set up are Federal and State.

A. $180,000; $25,800 B. $177,600; $29,700
C. $165,500; $20,000 D. $171,100; $30,000

44. In the examination of a manufacturing company where inventory values are of a material amount, the client has restricted the extent of the independent CPA's audit examination of his records by not permitting the CPA to observe the taking of inventory at the close of the company's fiscal year. In such a case, which of the following opinions with regard to the audit report would be APPROPRIATE?_______opinion. 44._____

A. Unqualified
B. Qualified
C. Adverse
D. Disclaimer of

45. Accounting data are subject to error from a variety of sources and for a variety of reasons. Of the following, the MOST efficient way to lessen this problem is to 45._____

A. identify'and classify errors as to type and kind as soon as they are detected
B. provide for machine calculation of accounting datawherever possible
C. confirm accounting data by independent third parties
D. designate an individual to be responsible for the accuracy of accounting data

46. Normally, an auditor does NOT rely upon his study and testing of a system of internal control to 46._____

A. evaluate the reliability of the system
B. uncover embezzlements of the client's system
C. help determine the scope of other auditing procedures to be followed
D. gain support for his opinion as to the accuracy and fairness of the financial statements

Questions 47-50.

DIRECTIONS: Questions 47 through 50 are to be answered on the basis of the information given below.

An office clerk who was not familiar with proper accounting procedures prepared the following financial report for the Dunrite Corporation as of June 30, 2018. In addition to the errors in presentation, additional data below were not considered in the preparationof the report. Restate this balance sheet in proper form, giving recognition to the additional data so that you will be able to determine the required information to answer these questions.

DUNRITE CORPORATION
June 30, 2018

CURRENT ASSETS			
Cash			$155,000
Marketable securities			82,400
Investment in affiliated company.			175,000
Treasury stock		$ 25,500	
Less reserve for trea		25,500	
Accounts receivable		$ 277,800	
Accounts payable		135,000	142,800
Total current assets			$555,200
PLANT ASSETS			
Equipment		$ 450,000	
Building	$400,000		
Reserve for plant expansion	100,000	300,000	
Land.		50,000	
Goodwill		35,000	
Prepaid expenses		12,000	847,000
Total Assets			$1,402,200

LIABILITIES			
Cash dividend payable		$ 25,000	
Stock dividend payable		15,000	
Accrued liabilities		15,700	
Bonds payable	$400,000		
Sinking fund	325,000	75,000	
Total Current Liabilities			$ 130,700
STOCKHOLDERS' EQUITY			
Paid-in capital			
Common stock		$550,000	
Retained earnings and reserves			
Premium common stock	$ 74,000		
Reserve - doubtful accounts	7,500		
Reserve - depreciation of equipment	140,000		
Reserve - depreciation building	170,000		
Reserve - income-taxes	50,000		
Retained earnings	280,000	$721,500	
Total Liabilities and Equity			$1,402,200

ADDITIONAL DATA:

A. The reserve for income taxes represents the balance due on the estimated liability for taxes on income of the current fiscal year.
B. Marketable securities are recorded at cost and have a market value at June 30, 2018 of $81,000. They represent temporary investments.
C. The investment in the affiliated company is a minority interest carried at cost.
D. Bonds payable are due 10 years from the balance-sheet date.
E. The stock dividend payable was declared on June 30, 2018.

47. After restatement of the balance sheet in proper form, and giving recognition to The additional data, the Total Current Assets would be 47.______
A. $509,200 B. $519,700 C. $610,000 D. $735,000

48. After restatement of the balance sheet in proper form, and giving recognition to the Additional data, the Total Current Liabilities would be 48.______
A. $225,700 B. $325,200 C. $352,700 D. $480,000

49. After restatement of the balance sheet in proper form, and giving recognition to the additional data, the Stockholders' Equity shows a total of 49.______
A. $730,100 B. $819,000 C. $910,000 D. $1,019,000

50. After restatement of the balance sheet in proper form, and giving recognition to the additional data, the net book value of the total plant equipment would be 50.______
A. $440,000 B. $590,000 C. $750,000 D. $850,000

KEY (CORRECT ANSWERS)

1. D
2. C
3. B
4. D
5. D
6. B
7. B
8. C
9. B
10. B
11. D
12. A
13. B
14. A
15. A
16. A
17. C
18. B
19. A
20. A
21. A
22. B
23. A
24. D
25. A
26. B
27. A
28. D
29. A
30. D
31. D
32. A
33. A
34. C
35. C
36. A
37. B
38. D
39. B
40. A
41. A
42. B
43. D
44. D
45. C
46. B
47. B
48. A
49. D
50. B

TEST 2

DIRECTIONS: Each question or incomplete statement is followed by several suggested answers or completions.Select the one that BEST answers the question or completes the statement. *PRINT THE LETTER OF THE CORRECT ANSWER IN THE SPACE AT THE RIGHT.*

Question 1.

DIRECTIONS: Question 1 is based on the following portion of an income tax withholding table. In answering this question, assume that this table was in effect for the full year.

If the payroll period with respect to an employee is daily:

And the wages are		And the number of witholding exemptions claimed is				
At least	But less than	0	1	2	3	4
		The amount of income tax to be withheld shall be				
$172	$176	$24.40	$20.80	$17.20	$13.60	$10.00
176	180	24.90	21.30	17.70	14.20	10.60
180	184	25.50	18.30	18.30	14.70	11.10

1. K received a daily wage of $176.40 the first 7 pay periods and $182.50 the last 19 pay periods. He claimed 3 exemptions the first 9 pay periods and 4 the rest of the year. Total income tax withheld during the year was 1._____
   A. $288.10 B. $295.30
   C. $316.50 D. $317.50
   E. none of the above

2. A voucher contained the following items: 2._____
   6 desks @89.20 $525.20
   8 chairs @32.50 260.00
   Total 885.20
   The terms were given on the voucher as 3%, 10 days; net, 30 days. Verify the computations, which may be incorrect, and calculate the correct amount to be paid. If payment is made within the discount period, the amount to be paid is
   A. $761.64 B. $771.34
   C. $795.20 D. $858.64
   E. none of the above

3. Under the income tax law in effect for last year, an individual who is blind on the last day of the taxable year is entitled to claim an exemption of $600 because of such blindness, in addition to any other exemptions to which he may be entitled. 3._____
   Richard Roe, who files his income tax returns on the calendar year basis, became permanently blind on December 15 of last year.
   In filing his income tax return for last year, Mr. Roe may claim an exemption for blindness of
   A. $300 B. $550
   C. $574 D. $600
   E. none of the above

4. The Jones Company had a merchandise inventory of $24,625 on January 1 of last year. During that year, purchases made by the company amounted to $60,000, sales to $85,065, and cost of goo ds sold to $28,060. 4.____
The inventory on December 31 of last year was
   A. $25,065
   B. $28,500
   C. $49,690
   D. $57,005
   E. none of the above

KEY (CORRECT ANSWERS)

1. D
2. B
3. D
4. E

ACCOUNTING

EXAMINATION SECTION

TEST 1

DIRECTIONS: Each question or incomplete statement is followed by several suggested answers or completions. Select the one that BEST answers the question or completes the statement. *PRINT THE LETTER OF THE CORRECT ANSWER IN THE SPACE AT THE RIGHT.*

Questions 1-5.

DIRECTIONS: Questions 1 through 5 are to be answered on the basis of the following information.

When balance sheets are analyzed, working capital always receives close attention. Adequate working capital enables a company to carry sufficient inventories, meet current debts, take advantage of cash discounts and extend favorable terms to customers. A company that is deficient in working capital and unable to do these things is in a poor competitive position.

Below is a Trial Balance as of June 30, 2021, in alphabetical order, of the Worth Corporation.

	Debits	Credits
Accounts Payable		$50,000
Accounts Receivable	$40,000	
Accrued Expenses Payable		10,000
Capital Stock		10,000
Cash	20,000	
Depreciation Expense	5,000	
Inventory	60,000	
Plant & Equipment (net)	30,000	
Retained Earnings		20,000
Salary Expense	35,000	
Sales		100,000
	$190,000	$190,000

1. The Worth Corporation's Working Capital, based on the data above, is 1.____
   A. $50,000 B. $55,000 C. $60,000 D. $65,000

2. Which one of the following transactions increases Working Capital? 2.____
   A. Collecting outstanding accounts receivable
   B. Borrowing money from the bank based upon a 90-day interest-bearing note payable
   C. Paying off a 60-day note payable to the bank
   D. Selling merchandise at a profit

3. The Worth Corporation's Current Ratio, based on the above data, is 3.____
   A. 1.7 to 1   B. 2 to 1   C. 2.5 to 1   D. 4 to 3

4. Which one of the following transactions decreases the Current Ratio? 4.____
   A. Collecting an account receivable
   B. Borrowing money from the bank giving a 90-day interest-bearing note payable
   C. Paying off a 60-day note payable to the bank
   D. Selling merchandise at a profit

5. The payment of a current liability, such as Payroll Taxes Payable, will 5.____
   A. *increase* the current ratio but have no effect on the working capital
   B. *increase* the Working Capital, but have no effect on the current ratio
   C. *decrease* both the current ratio and working capital
   D. *increase* both the current ratio and working capital

6. During the year 2021, the Ramp Equipment Co. made sales to customers totaling $100,000 that were subject to sales taxes of $8,000. Net cash collections totaled $92,000. Discounts of $3,000 were allowed. During the year 2021, uncollectible accounts in the sum of $2,000 were written off the books. 6.____
   The net change in accounts receivable during the year 2021 was
   A. $10,500   B. $11,000   C. $13,000   D. $13,500

7. The Grable Co. received a $6,000, 8%, 60-day note dated May 1, 2021 from a customer. On May 16, 2021, the Grable Co. discounted the note at 6% at the bank. 7.____
   The net proceeds from the discounting of the note amounted to
   A. $5,954.40   B. $6,034.40   C. $6,064.80   D. $6,080.00

8. In reviewing the customers' accounts in the Accounts Receivable Ledger for the entire year 2020, the following errors are discovered. 8.____
   - A sale in the amount of $500 to the J. Brown Co. was erroneously posted to the K. Brown Co.
   - A sales return of $100 from the Gale Co. was debited to their account.
   - A check was received from a customer, M. White and Co. in payment of a sale of $500 less 2% discount. The check was entered properly in the cash receipts book but was posted to the M. White and Co. account in the amount of $490.

   The difference between the controlling account and its related accounts receivable schedule amounts to
   A. $90   B. $110   C. $190   D. $210

9. Assume that you are called upon to audit a cash fund. You find in the cash drawer postage stamps and I.O.U.'s signed by employees, totaling together $425. 9.____
   In preparing a financial report, the $425 should be reported as
   A. petty cash   B. investments
   C. supplies and receivables   D. cash

10. On December 31, 2020, before adjustment, Accounts Receivable had a debit balance of $60,000 and the Allowance for Uncollectible Accounts had a debit balance of $1,000. 10.____
If credit losses are estimated at 5% of Accounts Receivable and the estimated method of reporting bad debts is used, then bad debts expense for the year 2020 would be reported as
A. $1,000 B. $2,000 C. $3,000 D. $4,000

Questions 11-12.

DIRECTIONS: Questions 11 and 12 are to be answered on the basis of the following information.

Accrued salaries payable on $7,500 had not been recorded on December 31, 2021. Office supplies on hand of $2,500 at December 32, 2021 were erroneously treated as expense instead of inventory. Neither of these errors was discovered or corrected.

11. These two errors would cause the income for 4021 to be 11.____
A. *understated* by $5,000 B. *overstated* by $5,000
C. *understated* by $10,000 D. *overstated* by $10,000

12. The effect of these errors on the retained earnings at December 31, 2021 would be 12.____
A. *understated* by $2,500 B. *overstated* by $2,500
C. *understated* by $5,000 D. *overstated* by $5,000

Questions 13-14.

DIRECTIONS: Questions 13 and 14 are to be answered on the basis of the following information.

Albano, Borrone, and Colluci operate a retail store under the trade name of ABC. Their partnership agreement provides for equaling sharing profits and losses after salaries of $5,000 to Albano, $10,000 to Borrone, and $15,000 to Colluci.

13. If the net income of the partnership (prior to salaries to partners) is $21,000, then Albano's share of the profits, considering all aspects of the agreement, is determined to be 13.____
A. $2,000 B. $3,000 C. $5,000 D. $7,000

14. The share of the profits that apply to Borrone, similarly, is determined to be 14.____
A. $2,000 B. $3,000 C. $5,000 D. $7,000

Questions 15-17.

DIRECTIONS: Questions 15 through 17 are to be answered on the basis of the following information.

The Kay Company currently uses FIFO for inventory valuation. Their records for the year ended June 30, 2021 reflect the following:

July 1, 2021 inventory	100,000 units @ 7.50
Purchases during year	400,000 units @ $8.00
Sales during year	350,000 units @ $15.00
Expenses exclusive of income taxes	$1,290,000
Cash balance on June 30, 2021	$250,000
Income tax rate	34%

Assume the July 1, 2021 inventory will be the LIFO Base Inventory.

15. If the company should change to the LIFO as of June 30, 2021, then their income before taxes for the year-ended June 30, 2021, as compared with the income FIFO method, will be 15.____
    A. *increased* by $50,000
    B. *decreased* by $50,000
    C. *increased* by $100,000
    D. *decreased* by $100,000

16. Assuming the given tax rate (45%), the use of the LIFO method will result in an approximate tax expense for fiscal 2021 of 16.____
    A. $45,000
    B. $50,000
    C. $72,000
    D. $94,500

17. Assuming the given tax rate (45%), the use of the LIFO inventory method compared with the FIFO method, will result in a change in the approximate income tax expense for fiscal year 2021 as follows: 17.____
    A. *Increase* of $22,500
    B. *Decrease* of $22,500
    C. *Increase* of $45,000
    D. *Decrease* of $45,000

18. An accountant in an agency, in addition to his regular duties, has been assigned to train a newly appointed assistant accountant. The latter believes that he is not being given the training that he needs in order to perform his duties. Accordingly, the MOST appropriate FIRST step for the assistant accountant to take in order to secure the needed training is to 18.____
    A. register for the appropriate courses at the local college as soon as possible
    B. advise the accountant in a formal memo that his apparent lack of interest in the training is impeding his progress
    C. discuss the matter with the accountant privately and try to discover what seems to be the problem
    D. secure such training informally from more sympathetic accountants in the agency

19. You have worked very hard and successfully helped complete a difficult audit of a large corporation doing business with your agency. Your supervisor gives you a brief nod of approval when you expected a more substantial degree of recognition. You are angry and feel unappreciated. 19.____

Of the following, the MOST appropriate course of action for you to take would be to

A. voice your displeasure to your fellow workers at being taken for granted by an unappreciative supervisor
B. say nothing now and assume that your supervisor's nod of approval may be his customary acknowledgment of efforts well done
C. let your supervisor know that he owes you something by repeatedly stressing the outstanding job you've done
D. ease off on your work quality and productivity until your efforts are finally appreciated

20. You have been assisting in an audit of the books and records of businesses as a member of a team. The accountant in charge of your group tells you to start preliminary work independently on a new audit. This audit is to take place at the offices of the business. The business officers have been duly notified of the audit date. Upon arrival at their offices, you find that their records and files are in disarray and that their personnel are antagonistic and uncooperative. Of the following, the MOST desirable action for you to take is to 20.____

A. advise the business officers that serious consequences may follow unless immediate cooperation is secured
B. accept whatever may be shown or told you on the grounds that it would be unwise to further antagonize uncooperative personnel
C. inform your supervisor of the situation and request instructions
D. leave immediately and return later in the expectation of encountering a more cooperative attitude

KEY (CORRECT ANSWERS)

1.	C	11.	C
2.	D	12.	A
3.	B	13.	A
4.	B	14.	D
5.	A	15.	B
6.	B	16.	C
7.	B	17.	B
8.	D	18.	C
9.	C	19.	B
10.	D	20.	C

TEST 2

DIRECTIONS: Each question or incomplete statement is followed by several suggested answers or completions. Select the one that BEST answers the question or completes the statement. *PRINT THE LETTER OF THE CORRECT ANSWER IN THE SPACE AT THE RIGHT.*

Questions 1-3.

DIRECTIONS: Questions 1 through 3 are to be answered on the basis of the following information.

The city is planning to borrow money with a 5-year, 7% bond issue totaling $10,000,000 on principle when other municipal issues are paying 8%.
Present value of $1 – 8% - 5 years -68057
Present value of annual interest payments – annuity 8% - 5 years – 3.99271

1. The funds obtained from this bond issue (ignoring any costs relating to issuance) would be, approximately, 1.____
   A. $9,515,390 B. $10,000,000 C. $10,484,620 D. $10,800,000

2. At the date of maturity, the bonds will be redeemed at 2.____
   A. $9,515,390 B. $10,000,000 C. $10,484,610 D. $10,800,000

3. As a result of this issue, the ACTUAL interest costs each year as related to the 7% interest payments will 3.____
   A. be the same as paid ($700,000)
   B. be more than $700,000
   C. be less than $700,000
   D. fluctuate depending on the market conditions

4. Following the usual governmental accounting concepts, the activities of a municipal employee retirement plan, which is financed by equal employer and employee contributions, should be accounted for in a(n) 4.____
   A. agency fund B. intragovernmental service fund
   C. special assessment fund D. trust fund

Questions 5-7.

DIRECTIONS: Questions 5 through 7 are to be answered on the basis of the following information.

The Balance Sheet of the JLA Corp. is as follows:

Current Assets	$50,000	Current Liabilities	$20,000
Other Assets	75,000	Common Stock	75,000
Total	$125,000	Retained Earnings	30,000
		Total	$125,000

5. The working capital of the JLA Corp. is 5.____
   A. $30,000 B. $50,000 C. $105,000 D. $125,000

6. The operating ratio of the JLA Corp. is 6.____
   A. 2 to 1 B. 2½ to 1 C. 1 to 2 D. 1 to 2½

7. The stockholders' equity is 7.____
   A. $30,000 B. $75,000 C. $105,000 D. $125,000

8. This question is based on the following figures taken from a set of books for the year ending June 30, 2021. 8.____

	Trial Balance Before Adjustments	Trial Balance After Adjustments
Commissions Payable	cr...	cr $1,550
Office Salaries	dr $9,500	dr $10,680
Rental Income	cr $4,300	cr $4,900
Accumulated Depreciation	cr $7,000	cr $9,700
Supplies Expense	dr $1,760	dr $1,200

As a result of the adjustments reflected in the adjusted trial balance, the net income of the company before taxes will be
   A. *increased* by $4,270
   B. *decreased* by $4,270
   C. *increased* by $5,430
   D. *decreased* by $5,430

9. This question is based on the following facts concerning the operations of a manufacturer of office desks. 9.____

Jan. 1, 2021	Goods in Process Inventory	4,260 units	40% complete
Dec. 31, 2021	Goods in Process Inventory	3,776 units	25% complete
Jan. 1, 2021	Finished Goods Inventory	2,630 units	
Dec. 31, 2021	Finished Goods Inventory	3,180 units	

Sales consummated during the year: 127,460 units

Assuming that all the desks are the same style, the number of equivalent complete units, manufactured during the year 2021 is
   A. 127,250 B. 127,460 C. 128,010 D. 131,510

Questions 10-11.

DIRECTIONS: Questions 10 and 11 are to be answered on the basis of the following information.

On January 1, 2021, the Lenox Corporation was organized with a cash investment of $50,000 by the shareholders. Some of the corporate records were destroyed. However, you were able to discover the following facts from various sources.

Accounts Payable at December 31, 2021 (arising from merchandise purchased)	$16,000
Accounts Receivable at December 31, 2021 (arising from the sales of merchandise)	$18,000
Sales for the calendar year 2021	$94,000
Inventory, December 31, 2021	20,000
Cost of Goods Sold is 60% of the selling price	
Bank loan outstanding – December 31, 2021	15,000
Expenses paid in cash during the year	35,000
Expenses incurred but unpaid as of December 31, 2021	4,000
Dividend paid	25,000

10. The CORRECT cash balance is 10.____
    A. $5,600 B. $20,600 C. $38,600 D. $40,600

11. The stockholders' equity on December 31, 2021 is 11.____
    A. $23,600 B. Deficit of $26,400
    C. $27,600 D. $42,400

Questions 12-13.

DIRECTIONS: Questions 12 and 13 are to be answered on the basis of the following facts developed from the records of a company that sells its merchandise on the installment plan.

Sales	Calendar Year 2020	Calendar Year 2021
Total volume of sales	$80,000	$100,000
Cost of Goods Sold	60,000	40,000
Gross Profit	$20,000	$60,000
Cash Collections		
From 2020 Sales	$18,000	$36,000
From 2021 Sales		22,000
Total Cash Collections	$18,000	$58,000

12. Using the deferred profit method of determining thee income from installment sales, the gross profit on sales for the calendar year 2020 was 12.____
    A. $4,500 B. $18,000 C. $20,000 D. None

13. Using the deferred profit method of determining the income from installment sales, the gross profit on sales for the calendar year 2021 was 13.____
    A. $22,000 B. $22,200 C. $60,000 D. None

Questions 14-15.

DIRECTIONS: Questions 14 and 15 are to be answered on the basis of the data developed from an examination of the records of Ralston, Inc. for the month of April 2021.

Beginning Inventory: 10,000 units @ $4.00 each

	Purchases		Sales
April 10	20,000 units @ $5 each	April 13	15,000 units @ $8 each
17	60,000 units @ $6 each	21	50,000 units @ $9 each
26	40,000 units @ $7 each	27	50,000 units @ $10 each

14. The gross profit on sales for the month of April, 2021, assuming that inventory is priced on the FIFO basis, is 14.____
    A. $330,000 B. $355,000 C. $395,000 D. $435,000

15. The gross profit on sales for the month of April 2021, assuming that inventory is priced on the LIFO basis is 15.____
    A. $330,000 B. $355,000 C. $395,000 D. $435,000

16. This question is to be answered on the basis of the data presented for June 30, 2021. 16.____

Balance per Bank Statement	$24,019.00
Balance per General Ledger	20,592.64
Proceeds of note collected by the bank which had not been recorded in the Cash account	4,000.00
Interest on note collected by the bank (no book entries made0	39.40
Debit memo for Bank charges for the month of May	23.50
Deposit in Transit (June 30, 2021)	2,144.00
Customer's check returned by the bank due to lack of funds	150.00
Outstanding checks – June 30, 2021	1,631.46
Error in recording check made by our bookkeeper – check cleared in the amount of $463.00 but entered in the bank book for $436.00	

If we wish to reconcile the bank and book balance so that the bank balance and the book balance are reconciled to a corrected balance, the corrected balance should be
    A. $20,592.64 B. $24,019.00 C. $24,531.54 D. $26,163.00

17. The Ateb Company has issued a $500,000 bond issue on January 2, 2021 at 8% interest, payable semi-annually, sold at par, with interest payable on June 30 and December 31. 17.____
    On September 30, 2021, at the close of the fiscal year of the Ateb Company, the interest expense accrual should reflect interest payable of, approximately,
    A. $10,000 B. $20,000 C. $40,000 D. $50,000

18. Assume that a new procedure requires that a particular and unvarying sequence of steps be followed in order to yield the desired data. You are assigned to be in charge of subordinates working with this procedure. 18.____

Which one of the following is MOST likely to impress subordinates with the importance of following the sequence of steps exactly as given?

A. Explain the consequences of error if the procedure is not followed.
B. Suggest how rewarding would be the feeling of finding errors before the supervisor catches them.
C. Indicate that independent verification of their work will be done by other staff members
D. Advise that upward career mobility usually results from following instructions exactly

19. It is essential for an experienced accountant to know approximately how long it will take him to complete a particular assignment because 19.____

A. his supervisors will need to obtain this information only from someone planning to perform the assignment
B. he must arrange his schedule to insure proper completion of the assignment consistent with agency objectives
C. he must measure whether he is keeping pace with others performing similar assignments
D. he must determine what assignments are essential and have the greatest priority within his agency

20. There are circumstances which call for special and emergency efforts by employees. You must assign your staff to make this type of effort. 20.____
Of the following, this special type of assignment is MOST likely to succeed if the

A. time schedule required to complete the assignment is precisely stated but is not adhered to
B. employees are individually free to determine the work schedule
C. assignment is clearly defined
D. employees are individually free to use any procedure or method available to them

KEY (CORRECT ANSWERS)

1.	A	11.	A
2.	B	12.	A
3.	B	13.	B
4.	D	14.	C
5.	A	15.	B
6.	B	16.	C
7.	C	17.	A
8.	B	18.	A
9.	A	19.	B
10.	B	20.	C

EXAMINATION SECTION

TEST 1

DIRECTIONS: Each question or incomplete statement is followed by several suggested answers or completions. Select the one that BEST answers the question or completes the statement. *PRINT THE LETTER OF THE CORRECT ANSWER IN THE SPACE AT THE RIGHT.*

1. The Donaldson Company's cash balance includes a sum of $1,200,000 appropriated by the Board of Directors for the purchase of new equipment. On its financial statements, this amount should be included on the 1.____
   A. balance sheet as a current asset
   B. balance sheet as a non-current asset, specifically identified
   C. balance sheet as a fixed asset, included as part of plant cost
   D. income statement as a non-operating expense

2. The trial balance of the Davis Corporation as of June 30, 2021, the end of its fiscal year, included opposite the title ESTIMATED FEDERAL INCOME TAXES ACCRUED the amount of $35,000, which included the company's estimate of the Federal income tax it would have to pay for its 2021 fiscal year and the amount of an unpaid additional assessment for the 2018 fiscal year. This amount should appear on the balance sheet as a(n) 2.____
   A. general reserve
   B. reduction of current assets
   C. current liability
   D. allocation of retained income

3. A weekly payroll check was issued to an hourly employee based upon 88 hours of work instead of the normal 38 hours. The time card was somewhat illegible, and the number looked like it could have been 88. The BEST control procedure to prevent such an error would be 3.____
   A. desk checking
   B. a hash total
   C. a limit test
   D. a code check

4. In preparing a bank reconciliation, outstanding checks should be 4.____
   A. *deducted* from the balance per books
   B. *deducted* from the balance per bank statement
   C. *added* to the balance per books
   D. *added* to the balance per bank statement

5. Independence is essential and is expected under the generally accepted auditing standards. The face and appearance of integrity and objectivity are BEST maintained if 5.____
   A. the auditor is unbiased
   B. the auditor is aware of the problem of third party liability
   C. there is no financial relationship between the client and the auditor
   D. all financial relationships between the auditor and the client are reported in footnote form

6. An audit program is a plan of action and is used to guide the auditor in planning his work. 6.____
Such a program, if standardized, must be modified to
   A. observe limits that management places on the audit
   B. counteract internal control weaknesses
   C. meet the limited training of the auditor
   D. limit interference with work of the firm being audited

7. In auditing the *Owner's Equity* section of any company, the section related to a publicly-held corporation which uses a transfer agent and registrar would be more intricate than the audit of a partnership. 7.____
Therefore, the procedure that an auditor should use in this case is to
   A. obtain a listing of the number of shares of securities outstanding
   B. make a count of the number of shareholders
   C. determine that all stock transfers have been properly handled
   D. count the number of shares of stock in the treasury

8. In recent years, it has become increasingly more important to determine the correct number of shares outstanding when auditing the owner's equity accounts. 8.____
This is TRUE because
   A. there has been more fraud with respect to securities issued
   B. there are increased complexities determining the earnings per share
   C. there are more large corporations
   D. the auditor has to test the amount of invested capital

9. In auditing corporation records, an auditor must refer to some corporate documents that are not accounting documents. 9.____
The one of the following to which he is LEAST likely to refer is
   A. minutes of the board of directors meeting
   B. articles of incorporation of the corporation
   C. correspondence with public relations firms and the shareholders
   D. the by-laws of the corporation

10. A generally accepted auditing procedure which has been required by AICPA requirements is the observation of inventories. 10.____
Since it is impossible to observe the entire inventory of a large firm, the auditor may satisfy this requirement by
   A. establishing the balance by the use of a gross profit percentage method
   B. using sampling procedures to verify the count made by the client
   C. accepting the perpetual inventory records, once he has established that the entries are arithmetically accurate
   D. accepting the management statement that the inventory is correct as to quantity where observation is difficult

11. Materiality is an important consideration in all aspects of an audit examination. Attention must be given to accounts with small and zero balances when examining accounts payable. 11.____
This does not conflict with the concept of materiality because

A. The size of a balance is no clue to possible understatement of a liability
B. the balance of the account is not a measure of materiality
C. a sampling technique may suggest examining those accounts under consideration
D. the total of the accounts payable may be a material amount and, therefore, no individual account payable should be eliminated from review

12. In establishing the amount of a liability recorded on the books, which of the following types of evidence should an auditor consider to be the MOST reliable? 12.____
A. A check issued by the company and bearing the payee's endorsement which is included with the bank statement
B. Confirmation of an account payable balance mailed by and returned directly to the auditor
C. A sales invoice issued by the client with a delivery receipt from an outside trucker attached
D. A working paper prepared by the client's accountant and reviewed by the client's controller

13. Prior period adjustments as defined by APIB Opinion #9 issued by the AICPA never flow through the income statement. 13.____
The one of the following which is NOT one of the four criteria established b APB #9 for meeting the qualifications for treatment as a prior period adjustment is that the adjustment item
A. is not susceptible to reasonable extension prior to the current period
B. must be determined primarily by someone other than company management
C. can be specifically identified with and directly related to the business activities of a particular prior period
D. when placed in the current period would give undesirable results of operations

14. The subject caption which does NOT belong in a report of a financial audit and review of operations of public agency is 14.____
A. Audit Program
B. Description of Agency Organization and Function
C. Summary Statement of Findings
D. Details of Findings

15. At the inception of an audit of a public assistance agency, you ascertain that the one-year period of your audit includes 240,000 serially numbered payment vouchers. 15.____
The sample selection which would enable you to render the MOST generally acceptable opinion on the number of ineligible persons receiving public assistance is
A. the number of vouchers issued in a one-month period
B. every hundredth voucher
C. a random statistical selection
D. an equal size block of vouchers from each month

16. Of the following, the one which BEST describes an internal control system is the 16.____
   A. division of the handling and recording of each transaction into component parts so as to involve at least two persons, with each performing an unduplicated part of each transaction
   B. expansion of the worksheet to include provisions for adjustments to the books of account prior to preparation of the financial statements
   C. recording of transactions affecting negotiable instruments in accordance with the principles of debit and credit, and giving these instruments special treatment if they are interest or non-interest bearing notes
   D. taking of discounts, when properly authorized by the vendor, as an incentive for prompt payment

17. During audits of small businesses, an accountant is less likely to find that these establishments have a system of internal control comparable to larger firms because small businesses GENERALLY 17.____
   A. can absorb the cost of small fraudulent acts which may be perpetrated
   B. benefit more than larger firms by prevention of fraud than by detection of fraud
   C. have limited staff and the costs of maintaining the system are high
   D. use a double entry system which serves as a substitute for internal control

18. In the performance of a financial audit, especially one where there is a need for a thorough knowledge of law, an accountant would BEST be advised to 18.____
   A. rely on the testimony of witnesses, as they may be found during the course of the audit, in preference to the written record
   B. rely on the presumption that the client's actions are illegal when the audit discloses meager facts or evidence
   C. be aware of the specific legal objectives he is attempting to attain by means of his audit
   D. be aware of different conclusions he can reach depending upon what facts are stressed or discounted in his audit

19. There are various types of budgets which are used to measure different government activities. 19.____
   The type of budget which PARTICULARLY measures input of resource as compared with output service is the _____ budget.
   A. capital B. traditional C. performance D. program

20. Bank balances are usually confirmed through the use of a standard bank confirmation form as authorized by the AICPA and the Bank Administration Institute. 20.____
   In addition to bank balances, these confirmations ALSO confirm
   A. the credit rating of the client
   B. details of all deposits during the past month
   C. loans and contingent liabilities outstanding
   D. securities held by the bank as custodian or the client

KEY (CORRECT ANSWERS)

1.	B	11.	A
2.	C	12.	B
3.	C	13.	D
4.	B	14.	A
5.	C	15.	C
6.	B	16.	A
7.	A	17.	C
8.	B	18.	C
9.	C	19.	C
10.	B	20.	C

TEST 2

DIRECTIONS: Each question or incomplete statement is followed by several suggested answers or completions. Select the one that BEST answers the question or completes the statement. *PRINT THE LETTER OF THE CORRECT ANSWER IN THE SPACE AT THE RIGHT.*

Questions 1-3.

DIRECTIONS: Questions 1 through 3 are based on the classification of items into the appropriate section of a corporation balance sheet. The list of sections to be used is given below:

Current Assets	Investments
Current Liabilities	Long-term Liabilities
Deferred Credits	Paid-in Capital
Deferred Expenses	Plant Assets
Intangible assets	Retained Earnings

1. With respect to *Bonds Payable Due* in 2021, the PROPER classification is 1.____
   A. Investments
   B. Paid-in Capital
   C. Retained Earnings
   D. Long-term Liabilities

2. With respect to *Premium on Common Stock*, the PROPER classification is 2.____
   A. Intangible Assets
   B. Investments
   C. Retained Earnings
   D. Paid-in Capital

3. With respect to *Organization Costs,* the PROPER classification is 3.____
   A. Intangible Assets
   B. Investments
   C. Plant Assets
   D. Current Liabilities

4. J. Frost operates a small, individually owned repair service and maintains adequate double entry records. A review of his bank accounts and other available financial records yields the following information: 4.____
   Deposits made during 2021 per bank statements totaled $360,000. Deposits included a bank loan of $25,000 and an additional investment by Frost of $5,000. Disbursements during 2021 per bank statements totaled $305,000. This amount includes personal withdrawals of $28,500 and repayment of debt of $15,000.
   The Net Equity of J. Frost at January 1, 2021 was determined to be $61,000. Net Equity of J. Frost at December 31, 2021 was determined to be $67,000. Based upon the *Net Worth* method, Frost's net income for the year ended December 31, 2021 was
   A. $6,000
   B. $29,500
   C. $41,500
   D. $55,000

Questions 5-8.

DIRECTIONS: Questions 5 through 8 are based on the following Balance Sheet, Income statement, and Notes relating to the books and records of the Hartman Corporation.

BALANCE SHEET (000 omitted)

	September 30, 2020 Debit	September 30, 2020 Credit	September 30, 2021 Debit	September 30, 2021 Credit
Cash	$18		$31	
Accounts Receivable	28		26	
Inventory	10		15	
Land	40		81	
Building and equipment (Net)	60		65	
Accounts Payable		$10		$11
Notes Payable		2		2
Bonds Payable		50		50
Mortgage Payable		20		46
Common Stock		50		86
Retained Earnings		24		23
	$156	$156	$218	$218

INCOME STATEMENT FOR FISCAL YEAR ENDING SEPTEMBER 30, 2021

Income:		
Sales		$85
Cost of Sales		40
Gross Margin		$45
Expenses:		
Depreciation	$5	
Loss on Sale of Fixed Assets	2	
Other Operating Expenses	32	
Total Expenses		$39
Net Income		$6

NOTES:

1. Dividend declared during the year 2021, $7,000
2. Acquired land; gave $36,000 common stock and cash for the balance.
3. Wrote off $1,000 accounts receivable and as uncollectible.
4. Acquired equipment; gave note secured by mortgage of $26,000.
5. Sold equipment; net cost per books, $16,000, sales price $14,000.

5. The amount of funds provided from net income for the year ended September 30 2021 is 5.____
   A. $6,000 B. $7,000 C. $13,000 D. $14,000

6. Financing and investing activities not affecting working capital are reported under the rules of APB #19. Notes 1 through 5 refer to various transactions on the books of the Hartman Corporation. 6.____
   Select the answer which refers to the numbers reflecting the concept mentioned here.
   A. Notes 1, 3, and 5 B. Notes 2 and 4
   C. Notes 2, 4, and 5 D. All five notes

7. Funds applied for the acquisition of the land are 7.____
   A. $5,000 B. $36,000 C. $41,000 D. None

8. The net change in working capital from 2020 to 2021 is 8.____
   A. $6,000 B. $16,000 C. $22,000 D. $35,000

9. Sales during July 2021 for the Magnum Corporation, operating in Los Angeles, were $378,000, of which $150,000 were on account. The sales figures given include the total sales tax charged to retail customers. (Assume a sales tax rate on all sales of 8%.) 9.____
   The CORRECT sales tax liability for July 2021 should be shown as
   A. $3,024 B. $18,240 C. $28,000 D. $30,240

10. Of the following statement ratios, the one that BEST represents a measure of cost efficiency is 10.____
   A. Acid Test Ratio
   B. Operating Costs to Net Sales Ratio
   C. Cost of Manufacturing to Plant Assets Radio
   D. Earnings Per Share

Questions 11-13.

DIRECTIONS: Questions 11 through 13 are to be answered on the basis of the following information:

An examination of the books and records of the Kay May Corporation, a machinery wholesaler, reveals the following facts for the year ended December 31, 2021:

a. Merchandise was sold and billed F.O.B. shipping point on December 31, 2021 at a sales price of $7,500. Although the merchandise costing $6,000 was ready for shipment on that date, the trucking company did not call for the merchandise until January 2, 2022. It was not included in the inventory count taken on December 31, 2021.

b. Merchandise with a sales price of $5,500 was billed and shipped to the customer on December 31, 2021. The merchandise costing $4,800 was not included in the inventory count taken on that day. Terms of sale were F.O.B. destination.

c. Merchandise costing $5,000 was recorded as a purchase on December 26, 2021. The merchandise was not included in the inventory count taken on December 31, 2021 since, upon examination, it was found to be defective and was in the process of being returned to the vendor.

d. Merchandise costing $2,500 was received on December 31, 2021. It was included in the inventory count on that date. Although the invoice was dated January 3, 2022, the purchase was recorded in the December 2021 Purchases Journal.

e. Merchandise costing $4,000 was received on January 3, 2022. It was shipped F.O.B. destination, and the invoice was dated December 30, 2021. The invoice was recorded in the December 2021 Purchases Journal, and the merchandise was included in the December 31, 2021 inventory.

11. The net change to correct the inventory value as of December 31, 2021 is: 11.____
    A. Increase $800 B. Increase $5,800
    C. Increase $6,800 D. Decrease $12,055

12. The net change to correct the sales figure for the year 2021 is: 12.____
    A. Increase $2,000 B. Decrease $5,500
    C. Decrease $7,500 D. $13,000

13. The net change to correct the purchases figure for the year 2021 is: 13.____
    A. Decrease $11,500 B. Decrease $4,000
    C. Decrease $5,000 D. Decrease $9,000

Questions 14-18.

DIRECTIONS: Each of the following Questions 14 through 18 consists of a description of a transaction that indicates a two-fold effect on the Balance Sheet. Each of these transactions may be classified under one of the following categories:

A. Assets are Understated, Retained Earnings are Understated
B. Assets are Overstated, Retained Earnings are Overstated
C. Liabilities are Understated, Retained Earnings are Overstated
D. Liabilities are Overstated, Retained Earnings are Understated

Examine each question carefully. In the correspondingly numbered space at the right, print the letter preceding the category above which BEST describes the effect of each transaction on the Balance Sheet as of December 31, 2021.

14. A major equipment purchase was made at the beginning of 2021. The equipment had an estimated six-year useful life, and depreciation was overlooked at December 31, 2021. 14.____

15. Unearned Rental Income was properly credited when received early in the year. No year-end adjustment was made to transfer the earned portion to an appropriate account. 15.____

16. Goods on hand at a branch office were excluded from the year-end physical inventory. The purchase of these goods had been properly recorded 16.____

17. Accrued Interest on Notes Receivable was overlooked as of December 31, 2021. 17.____

18. Accrued Federal Income Taxes for 2021 have never been recorded. 18.____

19. The following are account balances for the dates shown: 19.____

	Dec. 31, 2021	Dec. 31, 2020
Current Assets:		
Cash	$168,000	$60,000
Short-term investments	16,000	20,000
Accounts receivable (net)	160,000	100,000
Inventory	60,000	40,000
Prepaid expenses	4,000	40,000
Current Liabilities:		
Accounts payable	110,000	80,000
Dividends payable	30,000	0

Given the above account balances, the CHANGE in working capital is a(n)

A. increase of $128,000
B. decrease of $128,000
C. increase of $188,000
D. decrease of $188,000

20. In conducting an audit of plant assets, which of the following accounts MUST be examined in order to ascertain that additions to plant assets have been correctly stated and reflect charges that are properly capitalized? 20.____

A. Accounts receivable
B. Sales income
C. Maintenance and repairs
D. Investments

KEY (CORRECT ANSWERS)

1.	D	11.	A
2.	D	12.	B
3.	A	13.	D
4.	B	14.	B
5.	C	15.	D
6.	B	16.	A
7.	A	17.	A
8.	B	18.	C
9.	C	19.	A
10.	B	20.	C

EXAMINATION SECTION

TEST 1

DIRECTIONS: Each question or incomplete statement is followed by several suggested answers or completions. Select the one that BEST answers the question or completes the statement. *PRINT THE LETTER OF THE CORRECT ANSWER IN THE SPACE AT THE RIGHT.*

1. Gross income of an individual for Federal income tax purposes does NOT include 1.____
   A. interest credited to a bank savings account
   B. gain from the sale of sewer authority bonds
   C. back pay received as a result of job reinstatement
   D. interest received from State Dormitory Authority bonds

2. A cash-basis, calendar-year taxpayer purchased an annuity policy at a total cost of $20,000. Starting on January 1 of 2022, he began to receive annual payments of $1,500. His life expectancy as of that date was 16 years. 2.____
   The amount of annuity income to be included in his gross income for the taxable year 2022 is
   A. none B. $250 C. $1,250 D. $1,500

3. The transactions related to a municipal police retirement system should be included in a(n) _____ fund. 3.____
   A. intra-governmental service
   B. trust
   C. general
   D. special revenue

4. The budget for a given cost during a given period was $100,000. The actual cost for the period was $90,000. 4.____
   Based upon these facts, one should say that the responsible manager has done a better than expected job in controlling the cost if the cost is _____ budgeted production.
   A. variable and actual production equaled
   B. a discretionary fixed cost and actual production equaled
   C. variable and actual production was 90% of
   D. variable and actual production was 80% of

5. In the conduct of an audit, the MOST practical method by which an accountant can satisfy himself as to the physical existence of inventory is to 5.____
   A. be present and observe personally the audited firm's physical inventory being taken
   B. independently verify an adequate proportion of all inventory operations performed by the audited firm
   C. mail confirmation requests to vendors of merchandise sold to the audited firm within the inventory year
   D. review beforehand the adequacy of the audited firm's plan for inventory taking, and during the actual inventory-taking states, verify that this plan is being followed

Questions 6-7.

DIRECTIONS: Questions 6 and 7 are to be answered on the basis of the following information.

For the month of March, the ABC Manufacturing Corporation's estimated factory overhead for an expected volume of 15,000 lbs. of a product was as follows:

	Amount	Overhead Rate Per Unit
Fixed Overhead	$3,000	$.20
Variable Overhead	$9,000	$.60

Actual volume was 10,000 lbs. and actual overhead expense was $7,700.

6. The Spending (Budget) Variance was _____ (Favorable). 6.____
   A. $1,300 B. $6,000 C. $7,700 D. $9,000

7. The Idle Capacity Variance was 7.____
   A. $300 (Favorable) B. $1,000 (Unfavorable)
   C. $1,300 (Favorable) D. $8,000 (Unfavorable)

Questions 8-11.

DIRECTIONS: Questions 8 through 11 are to be answered on the basis of the following information.

A bookkeeper, who was not familiar with proper accounting procedures, prepared the following financial report for Largor Corporation as of December 31, 2021. In addition to the errors in presentation, additional data below was not considered in the preparation of the report. Restate this balance sheet in proper form, giving recognition to the additional data, so that you will be able to determine the required information to answer Questions 8 through 11.

LARGOR CORPORATION
December 31, 2021

Current Assets			
Cash		$110,000	
Marketable Securities		53,000	
Accounts Receivable	$261,400		
Accounts Payable	125,000	136,400	
Inventories		274,000	
Prepaid Expenses		24,000	
Treasury Stock		20,000	
Cash Surrender Value of Officers' Life Insurance Policies		105,000	$722,400
Plant Assets			
Equipment		350,000	
Building	200,000		
Reserve for Plant Expansion	75,000	125,000	
Land		47,500	
TOTAL ASSETS			$1,244,900

Liabilities			
Salaries Payable		16,500	
Cash Dividend Payable		50,000	
Stock Dividend Payable		70,000	
Bonds Payable	200,000		
Less Sinking Fund	90,000	110,000	
TOTAL LIABILITIES			$246,500
Stockholders' Equity:			
Paid In Capital			
Common Stock		350,000	
Retained Earnings and Reserves			
Reserve for Income Taxes	90,000		
Reserve for Doubtful Accounts	6,500		
Reserve for Treasury Stock	20,000		
Reserve for Depreciation Equipment	70,000		
Reserve for Depreciation Building	80,000		
Premium on Common Stock	15,000		
Retained Earnings	366,900	648,400	998,400
TOTAL LIABILITIES & EQUITY			1,244,900

Additional Data

A. Bond Payable will mature eight (8) years from Balance Sheet date.
B. The Stock Dividend Payable was declared on December 31, 2021.
C. The Reserve for Income Taxes represents the balance due on the estimated liability for taxes on income for the year ended December 31.
D. Advances from Customers at the Balance Sheet date totaled $13,600. This total is still credited against Accounts Receivable.
E. Prepaid Expenses include Unamortized Mortgage Costs of $15,000.
F. Marketable Securities were recorded at cost. Their market value at December 31, 2021 was $50,800.

8. After restatement of the balance sheet in proper form and giving recognition to the additional data, the Total Current Assets should be 8.____
A. $597,400 B. $702,400 C. $712,300 D. $827,300

9. After restatement of the balance sheet in proper form and giving recognition to the additional data, the Total Current Liabilities should be 9.____
A. $261,500 B. $281,500 C. $295,100 D. $370,100

10. After restatement of the balance sheet in proper form and giving recognition to the additional data, the net book value of plant and equipment should be 10.____
A. $400,000 B. $447,500 C. $550,000 D. $597,500

11. After restatement of the balance sheet in proper form and giving recognition to the additional data, the Stockholders Equity should be 11.____
A. $320,000 B. $335,000 C. $764,700 D. $874,700

12. When preparing the financial statement, dividends in arrears on preferred stock should be treated as a 12.____
    A. contingent liability B. deduction from capital
    C. parenthetical remark D. valuation reserve

13. The IPC Corporation has an intangible asset which it values at $1,000,000 and has a life expectancy of 60 years. 13.____
    The appropriate span of write-off, as determined by good accounting practice, should be _____ years.
    A. 17 B. 34 C. 40 D. 60

14. The following information was used in costing inventory on October 31: 14.____

October	1 -	Beginning inventory	800 units	@ $1.20
	4 -	Received	200 units	@ $1.40
	16 -	Issued	400 units	
	24 -	Received	200 units	@ $1.60
	27 -	Issued	500 units	

    Using the LIFO method of inventory evaluation (end-of-month method), the total dollar value of the inventory at October 31 was
    A. $360 B. $460 C. $600 D. $1,200

15. If a $400,000 par value bond issue paying 8%, with interest dates of June 30 and December 31, is sold in November 1 for par plus accrued interest, the cash proceeds received by the issuer on November 1 should be APPROXIMATELY 15.____
    A. $405,000 B. $408,000 C. $411,000 D. $416,000

16. The TOTAL interest cost to the issuer of a bond issue sold for more than its face value is the periodic interest payment _____ amortization. 16.____
    A. plus the discount B. plus the premium
    C. minus the discount D. minus the premium

17. If shareholders donate shares of stock back to the company, such stock received by the company is properly classified as 17.____
    A. Treasury stock B. Unissued stock
    C. Other assets – investment D. Current assets - investment

18. Assume the following transactions have occurred: 18.____
    1. 10,000 shares of capital stock of Omer Corp., par value $50, have been sold and issued on initial sale @ $55 per share during the month of June
    2. 2,000 shares of previously issued stock were purchased from shareholders during the month of September @ $58 per share.

    As of September 30, the stockholders' equity section TOTAL should be
    A. $434,000 B. $450,000 C. $480,000 D. $550,000

19. Mr. Diak, a calendar-year taxpayer in the construction business, agrees to construct a building for the Supermat Corporation to cost a total of $500,000 and to require about two years to complete. By December 31, 2021, he has expended $150,000 in costs, and it was determined that the building was 35% completed. 19.____
If Mr. Diak is reporting income under the completed contract method, the amount of gross income he will report for 2021 is
A. none B. $25,000 C. $175,000 D. $350,000

20. When the Board of Directors of a firm uses the present-value technique to aid in deciding whether or not to buy a new plant asset, it needs to have information reflecting 20.____
A. the cost of the new asset only
B. the increased production from use of new asset only
C. an estimated rate of return
D. the book value of the asset

KEY (CORRECT ANSWERS)

1.	D	11.	D
2.	B	12.	C
3.	B	13.	C
4.	A	14.	A
5.	D	15.	C
6.	A	16.	D
7.	B	17.	A
8.	C	18.	A
9.	C	19.	A
10.	B	20.	C

TEST 2

DIRECTIONS: Each question or incomplete statement is followed by several suggested answers or completions. Select the one that BEST answers the question or completes the statement. *PRINT THE LETTER OF THE CORRECT ANSWER IN THE SPACE AT THE RIGHT.*

Questions 1-3.

DIRECTIONS: Questions 1 through 3 are to be answered on the basis of the following information.

During your audit of the Avon Company, you find the following errors in the records of the company:

1. Incorrect exclusion from the final inventory of items costing $3,000 for which the purchase was not recorded.
2. Inclusion in the final inventory of goods costing $5,000, although a purchase was not recorded. The goods in question were being held on consignment from Reldrey Company.
3. Incorrect exclusion of $2,000 from the inventory count at the end of the period. The goods were in transit (F.O.B. shipping point); the invoice had been received and the purchase recorded.
4. Inclusion of items on the receiving dock that were being held for return to the vendor because of damage. In counting the goods in the receiving department, these items were incorrectly included. With respect to these goods, a purchase of $4,000 had been recorded.

The records (uncorrected) showed the following amounts:

1. Purchases, $170,000
2. Pretax income, $15,000
3. Accounts payable, $20,000; and
4. Inventory at the end of the period, $40,000.

1. The CORRECTED inventory is 1.____
   A. $36,000 B. $42,000 C. $43,000 D. $44,000

2. The CORRECTED income for the year is 2.____
   A. $12,000 B. $15,000 C. $17,000 D. $18,000

3. The CORRECT accounts payable liabilities are 3.____
   A. $16,000 B. $17,000 C. $19,000 D. $23,000

4. An auditing procedure that is MOST likely to reveal the existence of a contingent liability is 4.____
   A. a review of vouchers paid during the month following the year end
   B. confirmation of accounts payable
   C. an inquiry directed to legal counsel
   D. confirmation of mortgage notes

Questions 5-6.

DIRECTIONS: Questions 5 and 6 are to be answered on the basis of the following information.

Mr. Zelev operates a business as a sole proprietor and uses the cash basis for reporting income for income tax purposes. His bank account during 2021 for the business shows receipts totaling $285,000 and cash payments totaling $240,000. Included in the cash payments were payments for three-year business insurance policies whose premiums totaled $1,575. It was determined that the expired premiums for this year were $475. Further examination of the accounts and discussion with Mr. Zelev revealed the fact that included in the receipts were the following items, as well as the proceeds received from customers:

$15,000 which Mr. Zelev took from his savings account and deposited in the business account.

$20,000 which Mr. Zelev received from the bank as a loan which will be repaid next year.

Included in the cash payments were $10,000, which Mr. Zelev took on a weekly basis from the business receipts to use for his personal expenses.

5. The amount of net income to be reported for income tax purposes for calendar year 2022 for Mr. Zelev is 5.____
   A. $21,100 B. $26,100 C. $31,100 D. $46,100

6. Assuming the same facts as those reported above, Mr. Zelev would be required to pay a self-employment tax for 2022 of 6.____
   $895.05 B. $1,208.70 C. $1,234.35 D. $1,666.90

7. For the year ended December 2021, you are given the following information relative to the income and expense statements for the Sungam Manufacturers, Inc.: 7.____

Sales..		$1,000.000
Sales Returns...		95,000
Cost of Sales		
Opening Inventories	$200,000	
Purchases During the Year	567,000	
Direct Labor Costs	240,000	
Factory Overhead	24,400	
Inventories End of Year	235,000	

On June 5, 2021, a fire destroyed the plant and all of the inventories then on hand. You are given the following information and asked to ascertain the amount of the estimated inventory loss.

Sales up to June 15	$545,000
Purchased to June 15	254,500
Direct Labor	233,000
Overhead	14,550
Salvaged Inventory	95,000

The ESTIMATED inventory loss is
A. $96,000 B. $162,450 C. $189,450 D. $257,450

8. Losses and excessive costs with regard to inventory can occur in any one of several operating functions of an organization. 8.____
The operating function which bears the GREATEST responsibility for the failure to give proper consideration to transportation costs of material acquisitions is
A. accounting B. purchasing C. receiving D. shipping

Questions 9-17.

DIRECTIONS: Questions 9 through 17 are to be answered on the basis of the following information.

You are conducting an audit of the PAP Company, which has a contract to supply the municipal hospitals with specialty refrigerators on a cost-plus basis. The following information is available:

Materials Purchased	$1,946,700
Inventories, January 1	
Materials	268,000
Finished Goods (100 units)	43,000
Direct Labor	2,125,800
Factory Overhead (40% variable)	764,000
Marketing Expenses (all fixed)	516,000
Administrative Expenses (all fixed)	461,000
Sales (12,400 units)	6,634,000
Inventories, March 31	
Materials	167,000
Finished Goods (200 units)	(omitted)
No Work in Process	

9. The NET INCOME for the period is 9.____
A. $755,500 B. $1,237,500 C. $1,732,500 D. $4,980,500

10. The number of units manufactured is 10.____
A. 12,400 B. 12,500 C. 12,600 D. 12,700

11. The unit cost of refrigerators manufactured is MOST NEARLY 11.____
A. $389.00 B. $395.00 C. $398.00 D. $400.00

12. The TOTAL variable costs are 12.____
A. $305,600 B. $464,000 C. $4,479,100 D. $4,937,500

13. The TOTAL fixed costs are 13.____
A. $458,400 B. $1,435,400 C. $1,471,800 D. $1,741,000

While you are conducting your audit, the PAP Company advises you that they have changed their inventory costing from FIFO to LIFO. You are interested in pursuing the matter further because this change will affect the cost of the refrigerators. An examination of material part 2-317 inventory card shows the following activity:

May 2 – Received 100 units @ $5.40 per unit
May 8 – Received 30 units @ $8.00 per unit
May 15 – Issued 50 units
May 22 – Received 120 units @ $9.00 per unit
May 29 – Issued 100 units

14. Using the FIFO method under a perpetual inventory control system, the TOTAL cost of the units issued in May is 14.____
A. $690 B. $960 C. $1,590 D. $1,860

15. Using the FIFO method under a perpetual inventory control system, the VALUE of the closing inventory is 15.____
A. $780 B. $900 C. $1,080 D. $1,590

16. Using the LIFO method under a perpetual inventory control system, the TOTAL cost of the units issued in May is 16.____
A. $1,248 B. $1,428 C. $1,720 D. $1,860

17. Using the LIFO method under a perpetual inventory control system, the value of the closing inventory is 17.____
A. $612 B. $380 C. $1,512 D. $1,680

Questions 18-20.

DIRECTIONS: For Questions 18 through 20, consider that the EEF Corporation has a fully integrated cost accounting system.

18. Unit cost of manufacturing dresses was $7.00. Spoiled dresses numbered 400 with a sales value of $800. 18.____
When it is not customary to have a Spoiled Work account, the MOST appropriate account to be credited is
A. Work in Process B. Cost of Sales
C. Manufacturing Overhead D. Finished Goods

19. Overtime premium for factory workers (direct labor) totaled $400 for the payroll period. This was due to inadequate plant capacity. 19.____
The account to be DEBITED is
A. Work in Process B. Cost of Sales
C. Manufacturing Overhead D. Finished Goods

20. A month-end physical inventory of stores shows a shortage of $175. The account to be DEBITED to correct this shortage is 20.____
    A. Stores
    B. Work in Process
    C. Cost of Sales
    D. Manufacturing Overhead

KEY (CORRECT ANSWERS)

1.	A	11.	B
2.	A	12.	C
3.	C	13.	B
4.	C	14.	B
5.	A	15.	B
6.	D	16.	A
7.	B	17.	A
8.	B	18.	A
9.	A	19.	C
10.	B	20.	C

EXAMINATION SECTION
TEST 1

DIRECTIONS: Each question or incomplete statement is followed by several suggested answers or completions. Select the one that BEST answers the question or completes the statement. *PRINT THE LETTER OF THE CORRECT ANSWER IN THE SPACE AT THE RIGHT.*

Questions 1-2.

DIRECTIONS: Questions 1 and 2 are to be answered on the basis of the following information.

Your client, Oval Manufacturing, has several plants in different cities and serves customers in various other cities. Oval wants to know the best way to schedule shipments from various plants to various customers. You advise Oval that the problem can be solved by using the transportation method of linear programming.

1. In a transportation minimization problem, what are the usual coefficients of the objective function? 1.____

   A. Usage rates for transportation facilities
   B. Restrictions on transportation facilities
   C. Shipping costs
   D. Time estimates for the critical path

2. If the number of units at supply points exceeds the number of units demanded at destinations, what action should be taken concerning this inequality of supply and demand? 2.____

   A. Include a *dummy* demand equal to the excess supply
   B. Consider the excess supply to be a *dummy* supply
   C. Eliminate the excess supply
   D. Proceed without modification

Questions 3-6.

DIRECTIONS: Questions 3 through 6 are to be answered on the basis of the following information.

The following related entries were recorded in sequence in the general fund of a municipality:

1. Encumbrances	$12,000	
Reserve for encumbrances		$12,000
2. Reserve for encumbrances	12,000	
Encumbrances		12,000
3. Expenditures	12,350	
Vouchers payable		12,350

3. The sequence of entries indicates: 3.____

   A. An adverse event was foreseen and a reserve of $12,000 was created; later the reserve was cancelled and a liability for the item was acknowledged
   B. An order was placed for goods or services estimated to cost $12,000; the actual cost was $12,350, for which a liability was acknowledged upon receipt
   C. Encumbrances were anticipated but later failed to materialize and were reversed. A liability of $12,350 was incurred.
   D. The first entry was erroneous and was reversed; a liability of $12,350 was acknowledged

4. Entries similar to those for the general fund may also appear on the books of the municipality's 4.____

   A. general fixed-assets group
   B. general bonded-debt group
   C. trust fund
   D. special-revenue fund

5. Assuming appropriate governmental accounting principles were followed, the entries 5.____

   A. occurred in the same fiscal period
   B. did not occur in the same fiscal period
   C. could have occurred in the same fiscal period, but it is impossible to be sure of this
   D. reflect the equivalent of *a prior period adjustment* had the entity concerned been one operated for profit

6. Immediately after entry number one was recorded, the municipality had a balanced general fund budget for all transactions. 6.____
   What would be the effect of recording entries two and three?

   A. Not change the balanced condition of the budget
   B. Cause the municipality to show a surplus
   C. Cause the municipality to show a deficit
   D. Not affect the current budget but would affect the budget of the following fiscal period

7. The Cray Company reported sales of $2,000,000 in 2014 and $3,000,000 in 2015 made evenly throughout each year. The general price-level index during 2013 remained constant at 100; and at the end of 2014 and 2015, it was 102 and 104, respectively. 7.____
   What should Cray report as sales for 2015, restated for general price-level changes?

   A. $3,000,000
   B. $3,029,126
   C. $3,058,821
   D. $3,120,000

8. The following data were abstracted from the financial records of the Gauss Corporation for 2014: 8.____

Sales	$3,600,000
Bond interest expense	120,000
Income taxes	600,000
Net income	800,000

   How many times was bond interest earned in 2014?

   A. 6.67
   B. 7.67
   C. 11.67
   D. 12.67

9. The Molitor Company's merchandise inventories and other related accounts for 2014 follow: 9.____

Sales	$3,000,000
Cost of goods sold	2,200,000
Merchandise inventory:	
Beginning of year	500,000
End of year	600,000

Assuming that the merchandise-inventory buildup was relatively constant, how many times did the merchandise inventory turn over during 2014?

A. 4.00 B. 4.40 C. 5.00 D. 5.45

10. On July 18, 2013, the Amdor Corporation granted non-transferable options to certain of its key employees as additional compensation. The options permitted the purchase of 20,000 shares of Amdor's common stock at a price of $30 per share. On the date of grant, the market value of the stock was $42 per share. The options were exercisable beginning January 2, 2014, and expire on December 31, 2015. On February 3, 2014, when the stock was selling for $45 per share, all the options were exercised. How much total compensation should Amdor record from the issuance of these options? 10.____

A. $240,000 B. $300,000 C. $840,000 D. $900,000

11. For accounting purposes, the *operating cycle concept* 11.____

A. causes the distinction between current and non-current items to depend on whether they will affect cash within one year
B. permits some assets to be classified as current even though they are more than one year removed from becoming cash
C. has become obsolete
D. affects the income statement but not the balance sheet

12. Which of the following tables would show the LARGEST value for an interest rate of 5% for six periods? 12.____

A. Amount of 1 at compound interest
B. Present value of 1 at compound interest
C. Amount of annuity of 1 per period
D. Present value of annuity of 1 per period

13. Where a *general-purpose contingency reserve* has been set up in a prior fiscal year, how is the abolition of the *reserve* during the current fiscal year handled? 13.____

A. As a prior-period adjustment
B. By charging the *reserve* with the type of anticipated loss which occurred during the current fiscal year
C. As an extraordinary item
D. By charging the *reserve* and crediting retained earnings

14. What is the theoretically preferred method of presenting minority interest on a consolidated balance sheet? 14.____

A. As a separate item within the deferred-credits section
B. As a deduction from (contra to) goodwill from consolidation, if any
C. By means of notes or footnotes to the balance sheet
D. As a separate item within the stockholders' equity section

15. On a balance sheet, what is the preferable presentation of notes or accounts receivable from officers, employees, or affiliated companies? 15.____

A. As trade notes and accounts receivable if they otherwise qualify as current assets
B. As assets but separately from other receivables
C. As offsets to capital
D. By means of notes or footnotes

16. The ratio of earnings before interest and taxes to total interest expense is a measure of 16.____

A. liquidity
B. risk
C. activity
D. profitability

17. Which one of the following statements BEST describes cost allocation? 17.____

A. A company can maximize or minimize total company income by selecting different bases to allocate indirect costs.
B. A company should select an allocation base to raise or lower reported income on given products.
C. A company's total income will remain unchanged no matter how indirect costs are allocated.
D. A company, as a general rule, should allocate indirect costs randomly or based on an *ability-to-bear* criterion.

18. A small-scale representation of a business to predict the effect of alternate strategies is called a 18.____

A. critical path
B. decentralized unit
C. model
D. system

19. The mathematical notation for the total cost for a business is $2x^3 + 4x^2 + 3x + 5$, where x equals production volume. 19.____
Which of the following is the mathematical notation for the marginal cost function for this business?

A. $2(x^3 + 2x^2 + 1.5x + 2.5)$
B. $6x^2 + 8x + 3$
C. $2x^3 + 4x^2 + 3x$
D. $3x + 5$

20. Your client, a bank, is interested in knowing how many tellers to keep on duty during various times of the day. 20.____
What quantitative technique should this bank use?

A. PERT
B. Simplex algorithm
C. Dynamic programming
D. Queuing theory

KEY (CORRECT ANSWERS)

1. C
2. A
3. B
4. D
5. A
6. C
7. B
8. D
9. A
10. A
11. B
12. C
13. D
14. D
15. B
16. B
17. C
18. C
19. B
20. D

TEST 2

DIRECTIONS: Each question or incomplete statement is followed by several suggested answers or completions. Select the one that BEST answers the question or completes the statement. *PRINT THE LETTER OF THE CORRECT ANSWER IN THE SPACE AT THE RIGHT.*

Questions 1-3.

DIRECTIONS: Questions 1 through 3 are to be answered on the basis of the following information.

The following data have been abstracted from the financial statements of Hall, Inc., a calendar-year merchandising corporation:

Balance sheet data:	December 31, 2013	December 31, 2014
Trade accounts receivable - net	$ 84,000	$ 78,000
Inventory	150,000	140,000
Accounts payable - merchandise (credit)	(95,000)	(98,000)

- Total sales for 2014 were $1,200,000 and for 2013 were $1,100,000. Cash sales were 20% of total sales each year.
- Cost of goods sold was $840,000 for 2014.
- Variable general and administrative (G&A) expenses for 2014 were $120,000. They have varied in proportion to sales and have been paid 50% in the year incurred and 50% the following year.
  Unpaid G&A expenses are not included in accounts payable above.
- Fixed general and administrative expenses including $35,000 depreciation and $5,000 bad debt expense totaled $100,000 each year. The amount of such expenses involving cash payments was paid 80% in the year incurred and 20% the following year. Each year there were a $5,000 bad debt estimate and a $5,000 writeoff. Unpaid G&A expenses are not included in accounts payable above.

1. How much cash was collected during 2014 resulting from total sales in 2013 and 2014? 1.____

   A. $961,000
   B. $966,000
   C. $1,201,000
   D. $1,206,000

2. How much cash was disbursed during 2014 for purchases of merchandise? 2.____

   A. $818,700
   B. $827,000
   C. $838,500
   D. $847,000

3. How much cash was disbursed during 2014 for variable and fixed general and administrative expenses? 3.____

   A. $175,000
   B. $180,000
   C. $215,000
   D. $220,000

Questions 4-6.

DIRECTIONS: Questions 4 through 6 are to be answered on the basis of the following information.

On January 2, 2015, Easor Corporation leased some equipment to Easee Corporation. Both corporations are on a calendar year. This equipment had cost Easor $45,000. There were no other significant costs associated with the lease. Easor appropriately accounted for this transaction as a lease equivalent to a sale, and Easee appropriately treated it as a capitalized lease under an installment purchase. The lease is for a non-cancelable term of eight years with $10,000 rent payable at the beginning of each year. Easee made the first payment on January 2, 2015. The implicit interest rate is 10%, and the present value of an annuity of $1 in advance for eight years at 10% is $5.868. The *interest* method of amortization is used. The equipment is expected to have a ten-year life, no salvage value, and be depreciated on a straight-line basis.

4. What journal entry should Easor have made on January 2, 2015 to reflect the transaction as a lease equivalent to a sale? 4.____

		Debit	Credit
A.	Cash	$10,000	
	Investment in leased equipment	45,000	
	Unearned rental revenue		$10,000
	Equipment inventory		45,000
B.	Receivable	35,000	
	Cash	10,000	
	Equipment inventory		45,000
C.	Receivable	48,680	
	Cash	10,000	
	Cost of sales	45,000	
	Sales		58,680
	Equipment inventory		45,000
D.	Receivable	70,000	
	Cash	10,000	
	Cost of sales	45,000	
	Sales		80,000
	Equipment inventory		45,000

5. What journal entry should Easor have made on January 2, 2015, if this lease were to have been accounted for as an operating lease? 5.____

		Debit	Credit
A.	Cash	$10,000	
	Investment in leased equipment	45,000	
	Unearned rental revenue		$10,000
	Equipment inventory		45,000
B.	Receivable	35,000	
	Cash	10,000	
	Equipment inventory		45,000
C.	Receivable	$48,680	
	Cash	10,000	
	Cost of sales	45,000	
	Sales		$58,680
	Equipment inventory		45,000
D.	Receivable	70,000	
	Cash	10,000	
	Cost of sales	45,000	
	Sales		80,000
	Equipment inventory		45,000

6. Assume that Easee treated this transaction as an operating (true) lease rather than as a purchase of the equipment. By how much would 2015 income before income taxes differ between these two methods? 6.____

A. Zero B. $736 C. $4,132 D. $5,132

Questions 7-10.

DIRECTIONS: Questions 7 through 10 apply to the appropriate use of present-value tables. Given below are the present-value factors for $1.00 discounted at 8% for one to five periods. Each of the following items is based on 8% interest compounded annually from day of deposit to day of withdrawal.

Periods	Present value of $1 discounted at 8% per period
1	0.926
2	0.857
3	0.794
4	0.735
5	0.681

7. What amount should be deposited in a bank today to grow to $1,000 three years from today? 7.____

A. $\frac{\$1,000}{0.794}$
B. $1,000 x 0.926 x 3
C. ($1,000 x 0.926) + ($1,000 x 0.857) + ($1,000 x 0.794)
D. $1,000 x 0.794

8. What amount should an individual have in his bank account today before withdrawal if he needs $2,000 each year for four years with the first withdrawal to be made today and each subsequent withdrawal at one-year intervals? (He is to have exactly a zero balance in his bank account after the fourth withdrawal.) 8.____

A. $2,000 + ($2,000 x 0.926) + ($2,000 x 0.857) + ($2,000 x 0.794)
B. $\frac{\$2,000}{0.735} \times 4$
C. ($2,000 x 0.926) + ($2,000 x 0.857) + ($2,000 x 0.794) + ($2,000 x 0.735)
D. $\frac{\$2,000}{0.926} \times 4$

9. If an individual put $3,000 in a savings account today, what amount of cash would be available two years from today? 9.____

A. $3,000 x 0.857
B. $3,000 x 0.857 x 2
C. $\frac{\$3,000}{0.857}$
D. $\frac{\$3,000}{0.926} \times 2$

10. What is the present value today of $4,000 to be received six years from today? 10.____

A. $4,000 x 0.926 x 6
B. $4,000 x 0.794 x 2
C. $4,000 x 0.681 x 0.926
D. Cannot be determined from the information given

11. The Bartley Corporation acquired land, buildings, and equipment from a bankrupt company at a lump-sum price of $90,000. At the time of acquisition, Bartley paid $6,000 to have the assets appraised. The appraisal disclosed the following values: 11.____

Land	$60,000
Buildings	40,000
Equipment	20,000

What cost should be assigned to the land, buildings, and equipment, respectively?

A. $30,000, $30,000, and $30,000
B. $32,000, $32,000, and $32,000
C. $45,000, $30,000, and $15,000
D. $48,000, $32,000, and $16,000

12. The Ting Corporation acquired a 30% interest in the Ping Company on January 1, 2015 for $600,000. At that time, Ping had 2,000,000 shares of its $1 par value common stock issued and outstanding. During 2015, Ping paid cash dividends of $20,000 and thereafter declared and issued a 5% common stock dividend when the market value was $2 per share. Ping's net income for 2015 was $120,000. 12.____
What should be the balance in Ping's *Investment in Ting's Company* account at the end of 2015?

A. $570,000 B. $600,000 C. $630,000 D. $636,000

13. Mire Company acquired a 70% interest in the Tyre Company in 2013. For the years ended December 31, 2014 and 2015, Tyre reported net income of $80,000 and $90,000 respectively. During 2014, Tyre sold merchandise to Mire for $10,000 at a profit of $2,000. The merchandise was later resold by Mire to outsiders for $15,000 during 2015. For consolidation purposes, what is the minority interest's share of Tyre's net income for 2014 and 2015, respectively? 13.____

A. $23,400 and $27,600 B. $24,000 and $27,000
C. $24,600 and $26,400 D. $26,000 and $25,000

14. A quantitative technique used for selecting the combination of resources that maximizes profits or minimizes costs is 14.____

A. curvilinear analysis B. queuing theory
C. dynamic programming D. linear programming

15. A quantitative technique used to make predictions or estimates of the value of a dependent variable from given values of an independent variable(s) is 15.____

A. linear programming B. regression analysis
C. trend analysis D. queuing theory

16. A quantitative technique used to discover and evaluate possible cause-and-effect relationships is 16.____

A. linear programming
B. PERT
C. Poisson distribution models
D. correlation analysis

17. A formal diagram of the interrelationships of complex time series of activities is 17.____

A. PERT
B. the method of least squares
C. linear programming
D. Poisson distribution models

18. A quantitative technique which deals with the problem of supplying sufficient facilities to meet the needs of production lines or individuals that demand service unevenly is 18.____

A. regression analysis
B. PERT
C. queuing theory
D. curvilinear analysis

19. A sales office of Mast, Inc. has developed the following probability distribution for daily sales of a perishable product : 19.____

X (Units Sold)	P (Sales = X)
100	.2
150	.5
200	.2
250	.1

The product is restocked at the start of each day.
If the company desires a 90% service level in satisfying sales demand, the initial stock balance for each day should be

A. 250 B. 160 C. 200 D. 150

20. Stanley Company has 1,000,000 shares of common stock authorized with a par value of $3 per share, of which 300,000 shares are outstanding. Stanley authorized a stock dividend when the market value was $8 per share, entitling its stockholders to one additional share for each share held. The par value of the stock was not changed.
What entry, if any, should Stanley make to record this transaction? 20.____

A.	No entry		
B.	Retained earnings	$900,000	
	Common stock		$900,000
C.	Retained earnings	2,400,000	
	Common stock		900,000
	Capital in excess of par		1,500,000
D.	Stock dividend payable	900,000	
	Retained earnings	900,000	
	Common stock		1,800,000

KEY (CORRECT ANSWERS)

1.	C	11.	D
2.	B	12.	C
3.	A	13.	A
4.	C	14.	D
5.	A	15.	B
6.	B	16.	D
7.	D	17.	A
8.	A	18.	C
9.	C	19.	C
10.	C	20.	B

EXAMINATION SECTION

TEST 1

DIRECTIONS: Each question or incomplete statement is followed by several suggested answers or completions. Select the one that BEST answers the question or completes the statement. *PRINT THE LETTER OF THE CORRECT ANSWER IN THE SPACE AT THE RIGHT.*

1. Assume that a civil service list has been established for a position in an agency which had provisional appointees serving in three permanent vacancies. One of these provisionals is on the eligible list, but was discharged because permanent appointments were accepted by three eligibles who were higher on the list. The former provisional has complained to the agency head, alleging that special efforts were made to appoint these eligible. The personnel officer of the agency should advise the agency head that 1.____
   A. the court could compel them to appoint the former provisional appointee
   B. he is required by civil service law to appoint the higher ranking eligibles from the list
   C. the human rights commission could compel him to appoint the former provisional appointee
   D. he should attempt conciliation

2. Assume that two accountants working in a section under your supervision were appointed from the same eligible list. Accountant Jones received a higher score on the competitive examination than Accountant Doe; Jones was third on the eligible list and Doe was fifth. Jones was told to report to work on March 15 but Doe, who was working under a provisional appointment, was given permanent status as of March 1. For economic reasons, your agency head is considering abolishing one position of accountant and requests guidance from you before making any decision. 2.____
   It would be BEST to tell him that
   A. if he decides to abolish one position of accountant, he should lay off Jones because Doe was given permanent status before Jones
   B. under the rule of *one in three*, Doe could not have been reached for appointment before Jones, so that Doe would have to be laid off first
   C. if he decides to abolish one position of accountant, he should lay off Doe because Doe's provisional appointment was in violation of the Civil Service Law
   D. he should evaluate the performance of Jones and Doe before making any determination as to which accountant to lay off

3. An employee who has been on the job for a number of years became a problem drinker during the past year. The supervisor and this employee are good friends. 3.____
   Because this problem has been affecting the work of the unit adversely, it would be BEST for the supervisor to

A. attempt to cover up the problem by moving the subordinate's desk to a corner of the office where he would not be noticed so readily
B. refer the employee for counseling to the employee counseling service
C. reassign some of the problem drinker's responsibilities to other employees
D. send the employee home in a tactful manner whenever he reports for duty in an unfit condition

4. In a strike situation, a member of the striking union reports for work but abstains from the full performance of his duties in his normal manner. According to the state civil service law, it is ACCURATE to say that the 4.____
   A. employee should be presumed to have engaged in a strike
   B. employee should not be presumed to have engaged in a strike
   C. city must bear the burden of proving that the employee engaged in a strike
   D. city may deny the employee the opportunity to rebut any charge that he engaged in a strike

5. Assume that, as a manager in a health agency which is establishing a *management-by-objective* program, you are asked to review and make recommendations on the following goals set by the agency head for the coming year. 5.____
   Which one of these objectives should you recommend dropping because of difficulty in verifying the degree to which the goal has been attained?
   A. Establishing night clinics in two preventive health care centers
   B. Informing more people of available health services
   C. Preparing a training manual for data-processing personnel
   D. Producing a 4-page health news bulletin to be distributed monthly to employees

6. The MAIN purpose of the *management-by-objectives* system is to 6.____
   A. develop a method of appraising the performance of managerial employees against verifiable objectives rather than against subjective appraisals and personal supervision
   B. decentralize managerial decision-making more effectively by setting goals for personnel all the way down to each first-line supervisor as well as to staff people
   C. increase managerial accountability and improve managerial effectiveness
   D. enable top level managerial employees to impose quantitative goals which will focus attention on the relevant trends that may affect the future

7. Certain city and state employees are on one year's probation for violating the strike provisions of the state civil service law. 7.____
   According to a ruling by the state attorney general, in the event of layoffs during their year of probation, the status of these employees should be considered
   A. *permanent*, with retention rights based on original date of appointment
   B. *probationary*, subject to layoff before permanent employees

C. *permanent*, to be credited with one year less service than indicated by the original date of appointment
D. *probationary*, subject to layoff before other employees in the layoff unit except for those with one year's seniority

8. Assume that, as a senior supervisor conducting a training course for a group of newly assigned first-line supervisors, you emphasize that an effective supervisor should encourage employee suggestions. One member of the group dissents, asserting that many employees come up with worthless, time-wasting ideas. 8.____
The one of the following which would be the MOST appropriate response for you to make is that
A. the supervisor's attitude is wrong, because no suggestion is entirely without merit
B. the supervisor must remember that encouragement of employee suggestions is the major part of any employee development program
C. even if a suggestion seems worthless, the participation of the employee helps to increase his identification with the agency
D. even if a suggestion seems worthless, the supervisor may be able to save it for future use

9. The *grapevine* is an informal channel of communication which exists among employees in an organization as a natural result of their social interaction, and their desire to be kept posted on the latest information. Some information transmitted through the grapevine is truth, some half-truth, and some just rumor. 9.____
Which one of the following would be the MOST appropriate attitude for a member of a management team to have about the grapevine?
A. The grapevine often carries false, malicious, and uncontrollable rumors and management should try to stamp it out by improving official channels of communication.
B. There are more important problems; normally only a small percentage of employees are interested in information transmitted through the grapevine.
C. The grapevine can give management insight into what employees think and feel and can help to supplement the formal communication systems.
D. The grapevine gives employees a harmless outlet for their imagination and an opportunity to relieve their fears and tensions in the form of rumors.

10. Although there are no formal performance appraisal mechanisms for non-managerial employees, managers nevertheless make informal appraisals because some method is needed to measure progress and to let employees know how they are doing. 10.____
The MOST import recent trend in making performance appraisals is toward judging the employee primarily on the extent to which he has
A. tried to perform his assigned tasks
B. demonstrated personal traits which are accepted as necessary to do the job satisfactorily

C. accomplished the objectives set for his job
D. followed the procedures established for the job

11. The proof of a successful human relations program in an organization is the morale crises that never happen. 11.____
Of the following, the implication for managers that follows MOST directly from this statement is that they should
   A. review and initiate revisions in all organization policies which may have an adverse effect on employee morale
   B. place more emphasis on ability to anticipate and prevent morale problems than on ability to resolve an actual crisis
   C. see that first-line supervisors work fairly and understandingly with employees
   D. avoid morale crises at all costs, since even the best resolution leaves scar, suspicions, and animosities

12. Suppose that you are conducting a conference on a specific problem. One employee makes a suggestion which you think is highly impractical. 12.____
Of the following, the way for you to respond to this suggestion is FIRST to
   A. be frank and tell the employee that his solution is wrong
   B. ask the employee in what way his suggestion will solve the problem under discussion
   C. refrain from any comment on it, and ask the group whether they have any other solutions to offer
   D. ask another participant to point out what is wrong with the suggestion

13. Suppose that a manager notices continuing deterioration in the work, conduct, and interpersonal relationships of one of his immediate subordinates, indicating that this employee has more than a minor emotional problem. Although the manager has made an attempt to help this employee by talking over his problems with him on several occasions, the employee has shown little improvement. 13.____
Of the following, generally the MOST constructive action for the manager to take at this point would be to
   A. continue to be supportive by sympathetic listening and counseling
   B. show tolerance toward the performance of the disturbed employee
   C. discuss the employee's deteriorating condition with him and suggest that he seek professional help
   D. consider whether the need of this employee and the agency would be best served by his transfer to another division

14. A manager has a problem involving conflict between two employees concerning a method of performing a work assignment. He does not know the reasons for this conflict. 14.____
The MOST valuable communications method he can use to aid him in resolving the problem is
   A. a formal hearing for each employee
   B. a staff meeting

C. disciplinary memoranda
D. an informal interview with each employee

15. As a training technique, role-playing is generally considered to be MOST successful when it results in 15.____
A. uncovering the underlying causes of conflict so that any recurrences are prevented
B. recreating an actual work situation which involves conflict among people and in which members of the group simulate specific personalities
C. freeing some people from patterns of rigid thinking and enabling them to look at themselves and others in a new way
D. increasing the participants' powers of logic and reasoning

16. In conducting a disciplinary interview, a supervisor finds that he must ask some highly personal questions which are relevant to the problem at hand. 16.____
The interviewer is MOST likely to get truthful answers to these questions if he asks them
A. early in the interview, before the interviewee has had a chance to become emotional
B. in a manner so that the interviewee can answer them with a simple *yes* or *no*
C. well into the interview, after rapport and trust have been established
D. just after the close of the interview, so that the questions appear to be off the record

17. Suppose that, as a newly assigned manager, you observe that a supervisor in your division uses autocratic methods which are causing resentment among his subordinates. 17.____
Of the following, the MOST likely reason for this supervisor's using such methods is that he
A. was probably exposed to this type of supervision himself
B. does not have an intuitive sense of tact, diplomacy, and consideration and no amount of training can change this
C. received approval for use of such method from his former subordinates
D. does not understand the basic concept of rewards and punishment in the practice of supervision

18. A newly appointed employee, Mr. Jones, was added to the staff of a supervisor who, because of the pressure of other work, turned him over to an experienced subordinate by saying, *Show Mr. Jones around and give him something to do.* 18.____
On the basis of this experience, Mr. Jones' FIRST impression of his new position was most likely to have been
A. *negative*, mainly because it appeared that his job was not worth his supervisor's attention
B. *negative*, mainly because the more experienced subordinate would tend to emphasize the unpleasant aspects of the work
C. *positive*, mainly because his supervisor wasted no time in assigning him to a subordinate
D. *positive*, mainly because he saw himself working for a dynamic supervisor who expected immediate results

19. An employee who stays in one assignment for a number of years often develops a feeling of possessiveness concerning his knowledge of the job which may develop into a problem. 19.____
Of the following, the BEST way for a supervisor to remedy this difficulty is to
   A. give the employee less important work to do
   B. point out minor errors as often as possible
   C. raise performance standards for all employees
   D. rotate the employee to a different assignment

20. A supervisor who tends to be supportive of his subordinates, in contrast to a supervisor who relies upon an authoritarian style of leadership, is more likely, in dealing with his staff, to have to listen to complaints, to have to tolerate emotionally upset employees, and even have to hear unreasonable and insulting remarks. 20.____
Compared to the authoritarian supervisor, he is MORE likely to
   A. be unconsciously fearful of failure
   B. have an overriding interest in production
   C. have subordinates who are better educated
   D. receive accurate feedback information

KEY (CORRECT ANSWERS)

1.	B	11.	B
2.	B	12.	B
3.	B	13.	C
4.	A	14.	D
5.	B	15.	C
6.	C	16.	C
7.	B	17.	A
8.	C	18.	A
9.	C	19.	D
10.	C	20.	D

TEST 2

DIRECTIONS: Each question or incomplete statement is followed by several suggested answers or completions. Select the one that BEST answers the question or completes the statement. *PRINT THE LETTER OF THE CORRECT ANSWER IN THE SPACE AT THE RIGHT.*

1. Assume that one of your subordinates, a supervisor in charge of a small unit in your bureau, asks your advice in handling a situation which has just occurred in his unit. On returning from a meeting, the supervisor notices that Jane Jones, the unit secretary, is not at her regular work location. Another employee had become faint, and the secretary accompanied this employee outdoors for some fresh air. It is a long-standing rule that no employee is permitted to leave the building during office hours except on official business or with the unit head's approval. Quite recently another employee was reprimanded by the supervisor for going out at 10 A.M. for a cup of coffee. 1.____
Of the following, it would be BEST for you to advise the supervisor to
   A. circulate a memo within the unit, restating the department's regulation concerning leaving the building during office hours
   B. overlook this rule violation in view of the extenuating circumstances
   C. personally reprimand the unit secretary since all employees must be treated in the same way when official rules are broken
   D. tell the unit secretary that you should reprimand her, but that you've decided to overlook the rule infraction this time

2. Of the following, the MOST valid reason why the application of behavioral modification techniques to management of large organizations is not yet widely accepted by managers is these techniques are 2.____
   A. based mainly on research conducted under highly controlled conditions
   B. more readily adaptable to training unskilled employees
   C. incompatible with the validated *management-by-objectives* approach
   D. manipulative and incompatible with the democratic approach

3. Because of intensive pressures which have developed since the onset of the city's financial problems, the members of a certain bureau have begun to file grievances about their working conditions. These protests are accumulating at a much greater rate than normal and faster than they can be disposed of under the current state of affairs. Concerned about the possible effect of these unresolved matters on the productivity of the bureau at such a critical time, the administrator in charge decides to take immediate action to improve staff relations. 3.____
With this intention in mind, he should
   A. explain to the staff why their grievances cannot be handled at the present time; then inform them that there will be a moratorium on the filing of additional grievances until the current backlog has been eliminated
   B. assemble all grievants at a special meeting and assure them that their problems will be handled in due course, but the current pressures preclude the prompt settling of their grievances

C. assign the assistant directors of the bureau to immediately schedule and conduct hearings on the accumulated grievances until the backlog is eliminated
D. suggest that the grievants again confer with their supervisors about their problems, orally rather than in writing, with direct appeal to him for such cases as are not resolved in this manner

4. A supervisor is attending a staff meeting with other accounting supervisors during which the participants are to propose various possible methods of dealing with a complex operational problem. 4.____
The one of the following procedures which will MOST likely produce an acceptable proposal for solving this problem at this meeting is for the
A. group to agree at the beginning of the meeting on the kinds of approaches to the problem that are most likely to succeed
B. conference leader to set a firm time limit on the period during which the participants are to present whatever ideas come to mind
C. group to discuss each proposal fully before the next proposal is made
D. conference leader to urge every participant in the meeting to present at least one proposal

5. Which one of the following types of communication systems would foster an authoritarian atmosphere in a large agency? 5.____
A communication system which
A. is restricted to organizational procedures and specific job instructions
B. provides information to employees about the rationale for their jobs
C. informs employees about their job performance
D. provides information about the relationship of employees' work to the agency's goals

6. According to most management experts, the one of the following which would generally have SERIOUS shortcomings as a component of a performance evaluation program is 6.____
A. rating the performance of each subordinate against the performance of other subordinates
B. limiting the appraisal to an evaluation of current performance
C. rating each subordinate in terms of clearly stated, measurable job goals
D. interviewing the subordinate to discuss present job performance and ways of improvement

7. Which of the following is consistent with the management-by-objectives approach as used in a fiscal affairs division of a large city agency? 7.____
A. Performance goals for the division are established by the administrator, who requires daily progress reports for each accounting unit.
B. Each subordinate accountant participates in setting his own short-term performance goals.
C. A detailed set of short-term performance goals for each accountant is prepared by his supervisor.
D. Objectives are established and progress evaluated by a committee of administrative accountants.

Questions 8-11.

DIRECTIONS: Questions 8 through 11 are to be answered on the basis of the following information.

Assume that you are the director of a small bureau, organized into three divisions. The bureau has a total of twenty employees: fourteen in professional titles and six in clerical titles. Each division has a chief who reports directly to you and who supervises five employees.

For Questions 8 through 11, you are to select the MOST appropriate training method, from the four choices given, based on the situation in the question:

A. Lecture, with a small blackboard available
B. Lecture, with audio-visual aids
C. Conference
D. Buddy system (experienced worker is accompanied by worker to be trained)

8. A major reorganization of your department was completed. You have decided to conduct a training session of about one hour's duration for all your subordinates in order to acquaint them with the new departmental structure as well as the new responsibilities which have been assigned to the divisions of your bureau. 8.____

9. Three assistant supervisors, each with one year of service in your department, are transferred to your bureau as part of the process of strengthening the major activity of your bureau. In connection with their duties, if they are required to do field visits to business firms located in the various industrial areas of the city. 9.____

10. The work of your bureau requires that various forms be processed sequentially through each of three divisions. In recent weeks, you have received complaints from the division chiefs that their production is being impeded by a lack of cooperation from the chiefs and workers in the other divisions. 10.____

11. In order to improve the efficiency of the department, your department head has directed that all bureaus hold weekly, thirty-minute-long training sessions for all employees, to review relevant work procedures. 11.____

12. Which one of the following actions is usually MOST appropriate for a manager to take in order to encourage and develop coordination of effort among different units or individuals within an organization? 12.____
    A. Providing rewards to the most productive employees
    B. Giving employees greater responsibility and the authority to exercise it
    C. Emphasizing to the employees that it is important to coordinate their efforts
    D. Explaining the goals of the organization to the employees and how their jobs relate to those goals

13. The management of time is one of the critical aspects of any supervisor's performance. 13.____
Therefore, in evaluating a subordinate from the viewpoint of how he manages time, a supervisor should rate HIGHEST the subordinate who
   A. concentrates on each task as he undertakes it
   B. performs at a standard and predictable pace under all circumstances
   C. takes shortened lunch periods when he is busy
   D. tries to do two things simultaneously

14. A MAJOR research finding regarding employee absenteeism is that 14.____
   A. absenteeism is likely to be higher on hot days
   B male employees tend to be absent more than female employees
   C. the way an employee is treated as a definite bearing on absenteeism
   D. the distance employees have to travel is one of the most important factors in absenteeism

15. Of the following, the supervisory behavior that is of GREATEST benefit to the organization is exhibited by supervisors who 15.____
   A. are strict with subordinates about following rules and regulations
   B. encourage subordinates to be interested in the work
   C. are willing to assist with subordinates' work on most occasions
   D. get the most done with available staff and resources

16. In order to maintain a proper relationship with a worker who is assigned to staff rather than line functions, a line supervisor should 16.____
   A. accept all recommendations of the staff worker
   B. include the staff worker in the conferences called by the supervisor for his subordinates
   C. keep the staff worker informed of developments in the area of his staff assignment
   D. require that the staff worker's recommendations be communicated to the supervisor through the supervisor's own superior

17. Of the following, the GREATEST disadvantage of placing a worker in a staff position under the direct supervision of the supervisor whom he advises is the possibility that the 17.____
   A. staff worker will tend to be insubordinate because of a feeling of superiority over the supervisor
   B. staff worker will tend to give advice of the type which the supervisor wants to hear or finds acceptable
   C. supervisor will tend to be mistrustful of the advice of a worker of subordinate rank
   D. supervisor will tend to derive little benefit from the advice because to supervise properly he should know at least as much as his subordinate

18. One factor which might be given consideration in deciding upon the optimum span of control of a supervisor over his immediate subordinates is the position of the supervisor in the hierarchy of the organization. 18.____
It is generally considered proper that the number of subordinates immediately supervised by a higher, upper echelon, supervisor
A. is unrelated to and tends to form no pattern with the number of supervised by lower level supervisors
B. should be about the same as the number supervised by a lower level supervisor
C. should be larger than the number supervised by a lower level supervisor
D. should be smaller than the number supervised by a lower level supervisor

19. Assume that you are a supervisor and have been assigned to assist the head of a large agency unit. He asks you to prepare a simple, functional organization chart of the unit. 19.____
Such a chart would be USEFUL for
A. favorably impressing members of the public with the important nature of the agency's work
B. graphically presenting staff relationships which may indicate previously unknown duplications, overlaps, and gaps in job duties
C. motivating all employees toward better performance because they will have a better understanding of job procedures
D. subtly and inoffensively making known to the staff in the unit that you are now in a position of responsibility

20. In some large organizations, management's traditional means of learning about employee dissatisfaction has been in the *open door policy.* 20.____
This policy USUALLY means that
A. management lets it be known that a management representative is generally available to discuss employees' questions, suggestions, and complaints
B. management sets up an informal employee organization to establish a democratic procedure for orderly representation of employees
C. employees are encouraged to attempt to resolve dissatisfactions at the lowest possible level of authority
D. employees are provided with an address or box so that they may safely and anonymously register complaints

KEY (CORRECT ANSWERS)

1.	B	11.	A
2.	A	12.	D
3.	D	13.	A
4.	B	14.	C
5.	A	15.	D
6.	A	16.	C
7.	B	17.	B
8.	B	18.	D
9.	D	19.	B
10.	C	20.	A

EXAMINATION SECTION

TEST 1

DIRECTIONS: Each question or incomplete statement is followed by several suggested answers or completions. Select the one that BEST answers the question or completes the statement. *PRINT THE LETTER OF THE CORRECT ANSWER IN THE SPACE AT THE RIGHT.*

1. Which one of the following generalizations is MOST likely to be INACCURATE and lead to judgmental errors in communication? 1.____
   A. A supervisor must be able to read with understanding.
   B. Misunderstanding may lead to dislike.
   C. Anyone can listen to another person and understand what he means.
   D. It is usually desirable to let a speaker talk until he is finished.

2. Assume that, as a supervisor, you have been directed to inform your subordinates about the implementation of a new procedure which will affect their work. 2.____
   While communicating this information, you should do all of the following EXCEPT
   A. obtain the approval of your subordinates regarding the new procedure
   B. explain the reason for implementing the new procedure
   C. hold a staff meeting at a time convenient to most of your subordinates
   D. encourage a productive discussion of the new procedure

3. Assume that you are in charge of a section that handles requests for information on matters received from the public. One day, you observe that a clerk under your supervision is using a method to log-in requests for information that is different from the one specified by you in the past. Upon questioning the clerk, you discover that instructions changing the old procedure were delivered orally by your supervisor on a day on which you were absent from the office. 3.____
   Of the following, the MOST appropriate action for you to take is to
   A. tell the clerk to revert to the old procedure at once
   B. ask your supervisor for information about the change
   C. call your staff together and tell them that no existing procedure is to be changed unless you direct that it be done
   D. write a memo to your supervisor suggesting that all future changes in procedure are to be in writing and that they be directed to you

4. At the first meeting with your staff after appointment as a supervisor, you find considerable indifference and some hostility among the participants. 4.____
   Of the following, the MOST appropriate way to handle this situation is to
   A. disregard the attitudes displayed and continue to make your presentation until you have completed it
   B. discontinue your presentation but continue the meeting and attempt to find out the reasons for their attitudes

C. warm up your audience with some good-natured statements and anecdotes and then proceed with your presentation
D. discontinue the meeting and set up personal interviews with the staff members to try to find out the reason for their attitude

5. In order to start the training of a new employee, it has been a standard practice to have him read a manual of instructions or procedures. 5.____
This method is currently being replaced by the _____ method.
A. audio-visual
B. conference
C. lecture
D. programmed instruction

6. Of the following subjects, the one that can usually be successfully taught by a first-line supervisor who is training his subordinates is: 6.____
A. theory and philosophy of management
B. human relations
C. responsibilities of a supervisor
D. job skills

7. Assume that as supervisor you are training a clerk who is experiencing difficulty learning a new task. 7.____
Which of the following would be the LEAST effective approach to take when trying to solve this problem? To
A. ask questions which will reveal the clerk's understanding of the task
B. take a different approach in explaining the task
C. give the clerk an opportunity to ask questions about the task
D. make sure the clerk knows you are watching his work closely

8. One school of management and supervision involves participation by employees in the setting of group goals and in the sharing of responsibility for the operation of the unit. 8.____
If this philosophy were applied to a unit consisting of professional and clerical personnel, one should expect
A. the professional and clerical personnel to participate with equal effectiveness in operating areas and policy areas
B. the professional personnel to participate with greater effectiveness than the clerical personnel in policy areas
C. the clerical personnel to participate with greater effectiveness than the professional personnel in operating areas
D. greater participation by clerical personnel but with less responsibility for their actions

9. With regard to productivity, high morale among employees generally indicates a 9.____
A. history of high productivity
B. nearly absolute positive correlation with high productivity
C. predisposition to be productive under facilitating leadership and circumstances
D. complacency which has little effect on productivity

10. Assume that you are going to organize the professionals and clerks under your supervision into work groups or team of two or three employees. 10.____
Of the following, the step which is LEAST likely to foster the successful development of each group is to
   A. allow friends to work together in the group
   B. provide special help and attention to employees with no friends in their group
   C. frequently switch employees from group to group
   D. rotate jobs within the group in order to strengthen group identification

11. Following are four statements which might be made by an employee to his supervisor during a performance evaluation interview. 11.____
Which of the statements BEST provides a basis for developing a plan to improve the employee's performance?
   A. *I understand that you are dissatisfied with my work and I will try harder in the future.*
   B. *I feel that I've been making too many careless clerical errors recently.*
   C. *I am aware that I will be subject to disciplinary action if my work does not improve within one month.*
   D. *I understand that this interview is simply a requirement of your job and not a personal attack on me.*

12. Three months ago, Mr. Smith and his supervisor, Mrs. Jones, developed a plan which was intended to correct Mr. Smith's inadequate job performance. Now, during a follow-up interview, Mr. Smith, who thought his performance had satisfactorily improved, has been informed that Mrs. Jones is still dissatisfied with his work. 12.____
Of the following, it is MOST likely that the disagreement occurred because, when formulating the plan, they did NOT
   A. set realistic goals for Mr. Smith's performance
   B. set a reasonable time limit for Mr. Smith to effect his improvement in performance
   C. provide for adequate training to improve Mr. Smith's skills
   D. establish performance standards for measuring Mr. Smith's progress

13. When a supervisor delegates authority to subordinates, there are usually many problems to overcome, such as inadequately trained subordinates and poor planning. 13.____
All of the following are means of increasing the effectiveness of delegation EXCEPT:
   A. Defining assignments in the light of results expected
   B. Maintaining open lines of communication
   C. Establishing tight controls so that subordinates will stay within the bounds of the area of delegation
   D. Providing rewards for successful assumption of authority by a subordinate

14. Assume that one of your subordinates has arrived late for work several times during the current month. The last time he was late you had warned him that another unexcused lateness would result informal disciplinary action. If the employee arrives late for work again during this month, the FIRST action you should take is to 14.____
    A. give the employee a chance to explain this lateness
    B. give the employee a written copy of your warning
    C. tell the employee that you are recommending formal disciplinary action
    D. tell the employee that you will give him only one more chance before recommending formal disciplinary action

15. In trying to decide how many subordinates a manager can control directly, one of the determinants is how much the manager can reduce the frequency and time consumed in contacts with his subordinates. Of the following, the factor which LEAST influences the number and direction of these contacts is: 15.____
    A. How well the manager delegates authority
    B. The rate at which the organization is changing
    C. The control techniques used by the manager
    D. Whether the activity is line or staff

16. Systematic rotation of employees through lateral transfer within a government organization to provide for managerial development is 16.____
    A. *good*, because systematic rotation develops specialists who learn to do many jobs well
    B. *bad*, because the outsider upsets the status quo of the existing organization
    C. *good*, because rotation provides challenge and organizational flexibility
    D. *bad*, because it is upsetting to employees to be transferred within a service

17. Assume that you are required to provide an evaluation of the performance of your subordinates. Of the following factors, it is MOST important that the performance evaluation include a rating of each employee's 17.____
    A. initiative B. productivity C. intelligence D. personality

18. When preparing performance evaluations of your subordinates, one way to help assure that you are rating each employee fairly is to 18.____
    A. prepare a list of all employees and all the rating factors and rate all employees on one rating factor before going on to the next factor
    B. prepare a list of all your employees and all the rating factors and rate each employee on all factors before going on to the next employee
    C. discuss all the ratings you anticipate giving with another supervisor in order to obtain an unbiased opinion
    D. discuss each employee with his co-workers in order to obtain peer judgment of worth before doing any rating

19. A managerial plan which would include the GREATEST control is a plan which is 19.____
    A. spontaneous and geared to each new job that is received
    B. detailed and covering an extended time period
    C. long-range and generalized, allowing for various interpretations
    D. specific and prepared daily

20. Assume that you are preparing a report which includes statistical data covering increases in budget allocations of four agencies for the past ten years. 20.____
    For you to represent the statistical data pictorially or graphically within the report is a
    A. *poor* idea, because you should be able to make statistical data understandable through the use of words
    B. *good* idea, because it is easier for the reader to understand pictorial representation rather than quantities of words conveying statistical data
    C. *poor* idea, because using pictorial representation in a report may make the report too expensive to print
    D. *good* idea, because a pictorial representation makes the report appear more attractive than the use of many words to convey the statistical data

KEY (CORRECT ANSWERS)

1.	C	11.	A
2.	A	12.	B
3.	B	13.	C
4.	D	14.	A
5.	D	15.	D
6.	D	16.	C
7.	D	17.	B
8.	B	18.	A
9.	C	19.	B
10.	C	20.	B

TEST 2

DIRECTIONS: Each question or incomplete statement is followed by several suggested answers or completions. Select the one that BEST answers the question or completes the statement. *PRINT THE LETTER OF THE CORRECT ANSWER IN THE SPACE AT THE RIGHT.*

1. Research studies have shown that supervisors of groups with high production records USUALLY 1.____
   A. give detailed instructions, constantly check on progress, and insist on approval of all decisions before implementation
   B. do considerable paperwork and other work similar to that performed by subordinates
   C. think of themselves as team members on the same level as others in the work group
   D. perform tasks traditionally associated with managerial functions

2. Mr. Smith, a bureau chief, is summoned by his agency's head in a conference to discuss Mr. Jones, an accountant who works in one of the divisions of his bureau. Mr. Jones has committed an error of such magnitude as to arouse the agency head's concern. 2.____
   After agreeing with the other conferees that a severe reprimand would be the appropriate punishment, Mr. Smith SHOULD
   A. arrange for Mr. Jones to explain the reasons for his error to the agency head
   B. send a memorandum to Mr. Jones, being careful that the language emphasizes the nature of the error rather than Mr. Jones' personal faults
   C. inform Mr. Jones' immediate supervisor of the conclusion reached at the conference, and let the supervisor take the necessary action
   D. suggest to the agency head that no additional action be taken against Mr. Jones because no further damage will be caused by the error

3. Assume that Ms. Thomson, a unit chief, has determined that the findings of an internal audit have been seriously distorted as a result of careless errors. The audit had been performed by a group of auditors in her unit and the errors were overlooked by the associate accountant in charge of the audit. Ms. Thomson has decided to delay discussing the matter with the associate accountant and the staff who performed the audit until she verifies certain details, which may require prolonged investigation. 3.____
   Mrs. Thomson's method of handling this situation is
   A. *appropriate*; employees should not be accused of wrongdoing until all the facts have been determined
   B. *inappropriate*; the employees involved may assume that the errors were considered unimportant
   C. *appropriate*; employees are more likely to change their behavior as a result of disciplinary action taken after a *cooling off* period
   D. *inappropriate*; the employees involved may have forgotten the details and become emotionally upset when confronted with the facts

4. After studying the financial situation in his agency, an administrative accountant decides to recommend centralization of certain accounting functions which are being performed in three different bureaus of the organization
The one of the following which is MOST likely to be a DISADVANTAE if this recommendation is implemented is that 4.____
   A. there may be less coordination of the accounting procedure because central direction is not so close to the day-to-day problems as the personnel handling them in each specialized accounting unit
   B. the higher management levels would not be able to make emergency decisions in as timely a manner as the more involved, lower-level administrators who are closer to the problem
   C. it is more difficult to focus the attention of the top management in order to resolve accounting problems because of the many other activities top management is involved in at the same time
   D. the accuracy of upward and inter-unit communication may be reduced because centralization may require insertion of more levels of administration in the chain of command

5. Of the following assumptions about the role of conflict in an organization, the one which is the MOST accurate statement of the approach of modern management theorists is that conflict 5.____
   A. can usually be avoided or controlled
   B. serves as a vital element in organizational change
   C. works against attainment of organizational goals
   D. provides a constructive outlet for problem employees

6. Which of the following is generally regarded as the BEST approach for a supervisor to follow in handling grievances brought by subordinates? 6.____
   A. Avoid becoming involved personally
   B. Involve the union representative in the first stage of discussion
   C. Settle the grievance as soon as possible
   D. Arrange for arbitration by a third party

7. Assume that supervisors of similar-sized accounting units in city, state, and federal offices were interviewed and observed at their work. It was found that the ways they acted in and viewed their roles tended to be very similar, regardless of who employed them.
Which of the following is the BEST explanation of this similarity 7.____
   A. A supervisor will ordinarily behave in conformance to his own self-image.
   B. Each role in an organization, including the supervisory role, calls for a distinct type of personality.
   C. The supervisor role reflects an exceptionally complex pattern of human response.
   D. The general nature of the duties and responsibilities of the supervisory position determines the role.

8. Which of the following is NOT consistent with the findings of recent research about the characteristics of successful top managers? 8.____
   A. They are *inner-directed* and not overly concerned with pleasing others.
   B. They are challenged by situations filled with high risk and ambiguity.
   C. They tend to stay on the same job for long periods of time.
   D. They consider it more important to handle critical assignments successfully than to do routine work well.

9. As a supervisor, you have to give subordinates operational guidelines. 9.____
Of the following, the BEST reason for providing them with information about the overall objectives within which their operations fit is that the subordinates will
   A. be more likely to carry out the operation according to your expectations
   B. know that there is a legitimate reason for carrying out the operation in the way you have prescribed
   C. be more likely to handle unanticipated problems that may arise without having to take up your time
   D. more likely to transmit the operating instructions correctly to their subordinates

10. A supervisor holds frequent meetings with his staff. 10.____
Of the following, the BEST approach he can take in order to elicit productive discussions at these meetings is for him to
   A. ask questions of those who attend
   B. include several levels of supervisors at the meetings
   C. hold the meetings at a specified time each week
   D. begin each meeting with a statement that discussion is welcomed

11. Of the following, the MOST important action that a supervisor can take to increase the productivity of a subordinate is to 11.____
   A. increase his uninterrupted work time
   B. increase the number of reproducing machines available in the office
   C. provide clerical assistance whenever he requests it
   D. reduce the number of his assigned tasks

12. Assume that, as a supervisor, you find out that you often must countermand or modify your original staff memos. 12.____
If this practice continues, which one of the following situations is MOST likely to occur? The
   A. staff will not bother to read your memos
   B. office files will become cluttered
   C. staff will delay acting on your memos
   D. memos will be treated routinely

13. In making management decisions, the committee approach is often used by managers. 13.____
Of the following, the BEST reason for using this approach is to
   A. prevent any one individual from assuming too much authority
   B. allow the manager to bring a wider range of experience and judgment to bear on the problem

C. allow the participation of all staff members, which will make them feel more committed to the decisions reached
D. permit the rapid transmission of information about decisions reached to the staff members concerned

14. In establishing standards for the measurement of the performance of a management project team, it is MOST important for the project manager to 14.____
A. identify and define the objectives of the project
B. determine the number of people who will be assigned to the project team
C. evaluate the skills of the staff who will be assigned to the project team
D. estimate fairly accurately the length of time required to complete each phase of the project

15. It is virtually impossible to tell an employee either that he is not good as another employee or that he does not measure up to a desirable level of performance, without having him feel threatened, rejected, and discouraged. 15.____
In accordance with the foregoing observation, a supervisor who is concerned about the performance of the less efficient members of his staff should realize that
A. he might obtain better results by not discussing the quality and quantity of their work with them, but by relying instead on the written evaluation of their performance to motivate their improvement
B. since he is required to discuss their performance with them, he should do so in words of encouragement and in so friendly a manner as to not destroy their morale
C. he might discuss their work in a general way, without mentioning any of the specifics about the quality of their performance, with the expectation that they would understand the full implications of his talk
D. he should make it a point, while telling them of their poor performance, to mention that their work is as good as that of some of the other employees in the unit

16. Some advocates of management-by-objectives procedures in public agencies have been urging that this method of operations be expanded to encompass all agencies of the government, for one or more of the following reasons, not all of which may be correct: 16.____
I. The MBO method is likely to succeed because it embraces the practice of setting near-term goals for the subordinate manager, reviewing accomplishments at an appropriate time, and repeating this process indefinitely
II. Provision for authority to perform the tasks assigned as goals in the MBO method is normally not needed because targets are set in quantitative or qualitative terms and specific times for accomplishment are arranged in short-term, repetitive intervals
III. Many other appraisal-of-performance programs failed because both supervisors and subordinates resisted them, while the MBO approach is not instituted until there is an organizational commitment to it
IV. Personal accountability is clearly established through the MBO approach because verifiable results are set up in the process of formulating the targets

Which of the choices below includes ALL of the foregoing statements that are CORRECT?

A. I, III B. II, IV C. I, II, III, IV D. I, III, IV

17. In preparing an organizational structure, the PRINCIPAL guideline for locating staff units is to place them 17.____
   A. all under a common supervisor
   B. as close as possible to the activities they serve
   C. as close to the chief executive as possible without over-extending his span of control
   D. at the lowest operational level

18. The relative importance of any unit in a department can be LEAST reliably judged by the 18.____
   A. amount of office space allocated to the unit
   B. number of employees in the unit
   C. rank of the individual who heads the unit
   D. rank of the individual to whom the unit head reports directly

19. Those who favor Planning-Programming-Budgeting Systems (PPBS) as a new method of governmental financial administration emphasize that PPBS 19.____
   A. applies statistical measurements which correlate highly with criteria
   B. makes possible economic systems analysis, including an explicit examination of alternatives
   C. makes available scarce government resources which can be coordinated on a government-wide basis and shared between local units of government
   D. shifts the emphasis in budgeting methods to an automated system of data processing

20. The term applied to computer processing which processes data concurrently with a given activity and provides results soon enough to influence the selection of a course of action is _____ processing. 20.____
   A. realtime B. batch
   C. random access D. integrated data

KEY (CORRECT ANSWERS)

1.	D	11.	A
2.	C	12.	C
3.	B	13.	B
4.	D	14.	A
5.	B	15.	B
6.	C	16.	D
7.	D	17.	B
8.	C	18.	B
9.	C	19.	B
10.	A	20.	A

PREPARING WRITTEN MATERIAL

PARAGRAPH REARRANGEMENT COMMENTARY

The sentences that follow are in scrambled order. You are to rearrange them in proper order and indicate the letter choice containing the correct answer at the space at the right.

Each group of sentences in this section is actually a paragraph presented in scrambled order. Each sentence in the group has a place in that paragraph; no sentence is to be left out. You are to read each group of sentences and decide upon the best order in which to put the sentences so as to form a well-organized paragraph.

The questions in this section measure the ability to solve a problem when all the facts relevant to its solution are not given.

More specifically, certain positions of responsibility and authority require the employee to discover connection between events sometimes, apparently, unrelated. In order to do this, the employee will find it necessary to correctly infer that unspecified events have probably occurred or are likely to occur. This ability becomes especially important when action must be taken on incomplete information.

Accordingly, these questions require competitors to choose among several suggested alternatives, each of which presents a different sequential arrangement of the events. Competitors must choose the MOST logical of the suggested sequences.

In order to do so, they may be required to draw on general knowledge to infer missing concepts or events that are essential to sequencing the given events. Competitors should be careful to infer only what is essential to the sequence. The plausibility of the wrong alternatives will always require the inclusion of unlikely events or of additional chains of events which are NOT essential to sequencing the given events.

It's very important to remember that you are looking for the best of the four possible choices, and that the best choice of all may not even be one of the answers you're given to choose from.

There is no one right way to solve these problems. Many people have found it helpful to first write out the order of the sentences, as they would have arranged them, on their scrap paper before looking at the possible answers. If their optimum answer is there, this can save them some time. If it isn't, this method can still give insight into solving the problem. Others find it most helpful to just go through each of the possible choices, contrasting each as they go along. You should use whatever method feels comfortable and works for you.

While most of these types of questions are not that difficult, we've added a higher percentage of the difficult type, just to give you more practice. Usually there are only one or two questions on this section that contain such subtle distinctions that you're unable to answer confidently. And you then may find yourself stuck deciding between two possible choices, neither of which you're sure about.

EXAMINATION SECTION

TEST 1

DIRECTIONS: The sentences that follow are in scrambled order. You are to rearrange them in proper order and indicate the letter choice containing the correct answer. *PRINT THE LETTER OF THE CORRECT ANSWER IN THE SPACE AT THE RIGHT.*

1. Below are four statements labeled W, X, Y and Z. 1.____
   W. He was a strict and fanatic drillmaster.
   X. The word is always used in a derogatory sense and generally shows resentment and anger on the part of the user.
   Y. It is from the name of this Frenchman that we derive our English word, martinet.
   Z. Jean Martinet was the Inspector-General of Infantry during the reign of King Louis XIV.

   The PROPER order in which these sentences should be placed in a paragraph is:

   A. X, Z, W, Y B. X, Z, Y, W C. Z, W, Y, X D. Z, Y, W, X

2. In the following paragraph, the sentences, which are numbered, have been jumbled. 2.____
   I. Since then it has undergone changes.
   II. It was incorporated in 1955 under the laws of the State of New York.
   III. Its primary purposes, a cleaner city, has, however, remained the same.
   IV. The Citizens Committee works in cooperation with the Mayor's Inter-departmental Committee for a Clean City. 3.____

   The order in which these sentences should be arranged to form a well-organized paragraph is:

   A. II, IV, I, III B. III, IV, I, II C. IV, II, I, III D. IV, III, II, I

Questions 3-5.

DIRECTIONS: The sentences listed below are part of a meaningful paragraph but they are not given in their proper order. You are to decide what would be the BEST order in which to put the sentences so as to form a well-organized paragraph. Each sentence has a place in the paragraph; there are no extra sentences. You are then to answer Questions 3 through 5 inclusive on the basis of your rearrangements of these scrambled sentences into a properly organized paragraph.

In 1887 some insurance companies organized an Inspection Department to advise their clients on all phases of fire prevention and protection. Probably this has been due to the smaller annual fire losses in Great Britain than in the United States. It tests various fire prevention devices and appliances and determines manufacturing hazards and their safeguards. Fire research began earlier in the United States and is more advanced than in Great Britain. Later they established a laboratory specializing in electrical, mechanical, hydraulic, and chemical fields.

3. When the five sentences are arranged in proper order, the paragraph starts with the sentence which begins 3.____
   A. "In 1887..." B. "Probably this..." C. "It tests..."
   D. "Fire research..." E. "Later they..."

4. In the last sentence listed above, "they" refers to 4.____
   A. the insurance companies B. the United States and Great Britain
   C. the Inspection Department D. clients
   E. technicians

5. When the above paragraph is properly arranged, it ends with the words 5.____
   A. "...and protection." B. "...the United States."
   C. "...their safeguards." D. "...in Great Britain."
   E. "...chemical fields."

KEY (CORRECT ANSWERS)

1. C
2. C
3. D
4. A
5. C

TEST 2

DIRECTIONS: In each of the questions numbered I through V, several sentences are given. For each question, choose as your answer the group of number that represents the MOST logical order of these sentences if they were arranged in paragraph form. *PRINT THE LETTER OF THE CORRECT ANSWER IN THE SPACE AT THE RIGHT.*

1. I. It is established when one shows that the landlord has prevented the tenant's enjoyment of his interest in the property leased. 1.____
   II. Constructive eviction is the result of a breach of the covenant of quiet enjoyment implied in all leases.
   III. In some parts of the United States, it is not complete until the tenant vacates within a reasonable time.
   IV. Generally, the acts must be of such serious and permanent character as to deny the tenant the enjoyment of his possessing rights.
   V. In this event, upon abandonment of the premises, the tenant's liability for that ceases.

   The CORRECT answer is:
   A. II, I, IV, III, V
   B. V, II, III, I, IV
   C. IV, III, I, II, V
   D. I, III, V, IV, II

2. I. The powerlessness before private and public authorities that is the typical experience of the slum tenant is reminiscent of the situation of blue-collar workers all through the nineteenth century. 2.____
   II. Similarly, in recent years, this chapter of history has been reopened by anti-poverty groups which have attempted to organize slum tenants to enable them to bargain collectively with their landlords about the conditions of their tenancies.
   III. It is familiar history that many of the worker remedied their condition by joining together and presenting their demands collectively.
   IV. Like the workers, tenants are forced by the conditions of modern life into substantial dependence on these who possess great political aid and economic power.
   V. What's more, the very fact of dependence coupled with an absence of education and self-confidence makes them hesitant and unable to stand up for what they need from those in power.

   The CORRECT answer is:
   A. V, IV, I, II, III
   B. II, III, I, V, IV
   C. III, I, V, IV, II
   D. I, IV, V, III, II

3. I. A railroad, for example, when not acting as a common carrier may contract away responsibility for its own negligence. 3.____
   II. As to a landlord, however, no decision has been found relating to the legal effect of a clause shifting the statutory duty of repair to the tenant.
   III. The courts have not passed on the validity of clauses relieving the landlord of this duty and liability.
   IV. They have, however, upheld the validity of exculpatory clauses in other types of contracts.

V. Housing regulations impose a duty upon the landlord to maintain leased premises in safe condition.
VI. As another example, a bailee may limit his liability except for gross negligence, willful acts, or fraud.

The CORRECT answer is:
A. II, I, VI, IV, III, V
B. I, III, IV, V, VI, II
C. III, V, I, IV, II, VI
D. V, III, IV, I, VI, II

4. I. Since there are only samples in the building, retail or consumer sales are generally eschewed by mart occupants, and in some instances, rigid controls are maintained to limit entrance to the mart only to those persons engaged in retailing. 4.____
II. Since World War I, in many larger cities, there has developed a new type of property, called the mart building.
III. It can, therefore, be used by wholesalers and jobbers for the display of sample merchandise.
IV. This type of building is most frequently a multi-storied, finished interior property which is a cross between a retail arcade and a loft building.
V. This limitation enables the mart occupants to ship the orders from another location after the retailer or dealer makes his selection from the samples.

The CORRECT answer is:
A. II, IV, III, I, V
B. IV, III, V, I, II
C. I, III, II, IV, V
D. I, IV, II, III, V

5. I. In general, staff-line friction reduces the distinctive contribution of staff personnel. 5.____
II. The conflicts, however, introduce an uncontrolled element into the managerial system.
III. On the other hand, the natural resistance of the line to staff innovations probably usefully restrains over-eager efforts to apply untested procedures on a large scale.
IV. Under such conditions, it is difficult to know when valuable ideas are being sacrificed.
V. The relatively weak position of staff, requiring accommodation to the line, tends to restrict their ability to engage in free, experimental innovation.

The CORRECT answer is:
A. IV, II, III, I, V
B. I, V, III, II, IV
C. V, III, I, II, IV
D. II, I, IV, V, III

KEY (CORRECT ANSWERS)

1. A
2. D
3. D
4. A
5. B

TEST 3

DIRECTIONS: Questions 1 through 4 consist of six sentences which can be arranged in a logical sequence. For each question, select the choice which places the numbered sentences in the MOST logical sequent. *PRINT THE LETTER OF THE CORRECT ANSWER IN THE SPACE AT THE RIGHT.*

1. I. The burden of proof as to each issue is determined before trial and remains upon the same party throughout the trial. 1.____
   II. The jury is at liberty to believe one witness' testimony as against a number of contradictory witnesses.
   III. In a civil case, the party bearing the burden of proof is required to prove his contention by a fair preponderance of the evidence.
   IV. However, it must be noted that a fair preponderance of evidence does not necessarily mean a greater number of witnesses.
   V. The burden of proof is the burden which rests upon one of the parties to an action to persuade the trier of the facts, generally the jury, that a proposition he asserts is true.
   VI. If the evidence is equally balanced, or if it leaves the jury in such doubt as to be unable to decide the controversy either way, judgment must be given against the party upon whom the burden of proof rests.

   The CORRECT answer is:
   A. III, II, V, IV, I, VI
   B. I, II, VI, V, III, IV
   C. III, IV, V, I, II, VI
   D. V, I, III, VI, IV, II

2. I. If a parent is without assets and is unemployed, he cannot be convicted of the crime of non-support of a child. 2.____
   II. The term "sufficient ability" has been held to mean sufficient financial ability.
   III. It does not matter if his unemployment is by choice or unavoidable circumstances.
   IV. If he fails to take any steps at all, he may be liable to prosecution for endangering the welfare of a child.
   V. Under the penal law, a parent is responsible for the support of his minor child only if the parent is "of sufficient ability."
   VI. An indigent parent may meet his obligation by borrowing money or by seeking aid under the provisions of the Social Welfare Law.

   The CORRECT answer is:
   A. VI, I, V, III, II, IV
   B. I, III, V, II, IV, VI
   C. V, II, I, III, VI, IV
   D. I, VI, IV, V, II, III

3. I. Consider, for example, the case of a rabble rouser who urges a group of twenty people to go out and break the windows of a nearby factory. 3.____
   II. Therefore, the law fills the indicated gap with the crime of inciting to riot.
   III. A person is considered guilty of inciting to riot when he urges ten or more persons to engage in tumultuous and violent conduct of a kind likely to create public alarm.
   IV. However, if he has not obtained the cooperation of at least four people, he cannot be charged with unlawful assembly.

V. The charge of inciting to riot was added to the law to cover types of conduct which cannot be classified as either the crime of "riot" or the crime of "unlawful assembly."
VI. If he acquires the acquiescence of at least four of them, he is guilty of unlawful assembly even if the project does not materialize.

The CORRECT answer is:
A. III, V, I, VI, IV, II
B. V, I, IV, VI, II, III
C. III, IV, I, V, II, VI
D. V, I, IV, VI, III, II

4. I. If, however, the rebuttal evidence presents an issue of credibility, it is for the jury to determine whether the presumption has, in fact, been destroyed. 4.____
II. Once sufficient evidence to the contrary is introduced, the presumption disappears from the trial.
III. The effect of a presumption is to place the burden upon the adversary to come forward with evidence to rebut the presumption.
IV. When a presumption is overcome and ceases to exist in the case, the fact or facts which gave rise to the presumption still remain.
V. Whether a presumption has been overcome is ordinarily a question for the court.
VI. Such information may furnish a basis for a logical inference.

The CORRECT answer is:
A. IV, VI, II, V, I, III
B. III, II, V, I, IV, VI
C. V, III, VI, IV, II, I
D. V, IV, I, II, VI, III

KEY (CORRECT ANSWERS)

1. D
2. C
3. A
4. B

PREPARING WRITTEN MATERIAL

EXAMINATION SECTION

TEST 1

DIRECTIONS: Each of the sentences in this test may be classified under one of the following four categories:

A. *Incorrect* because of faulty grammar or sentence structure
B. *Incorrect* because of faulty punctuation
C. *Incorrect* because of faulty capitalization
D. *Correct*

Examine each sentence carefully to determine under which of the above four options it is best classified. Then, in the space at the right, print the capital letter preceding the option which is the BEST of the four suggested above.

(Each incorrect sentence contains but one type of error. Consider a sentence to be correct if it contains none of the types of errors mentioned, even though there may be other correct ways of expressing the same thought.)

1. This fact, together with those brought out at the previous meeting, prove that the schedule is satisfactory to the employees. 1.____

2. Like many employees in scientific fields, the work of bookkeepers and accountants requires accuracy and neatness. 2.____

3. "What can I do for you," the secretary asked as she motioned to the visitor to take a seat. 3.____

4. Our representative, Mr. Charles will call on you next week to determine whether or not your claim has merit. 4.____

5. We expect you to return in the spring; please do not disappoint us. 5.____

6. Any supervisor, who disregards the just complaints of his subordinates, is remiss in the performance of his duty. 6.____

7. Because she took less than an hour for lunch is no reason for permitting her to leave before five o'clock. 7.____

8. "Miss Smith," said the supervisor, "Please arrange a meeting of the staff for two o'clock on Monday." 8.____

9. A private company's vacation and sick leave allowance usually differs considerably from a public agency. 9.____

10. Therefore, in order to increase the efficiency of operations in the department, a report on the recommended changes in procedures was presented to the departmental committee in charge of the program. 10.____

11. We told him to assign the work to whoever was available. 11.____

12. Since John was the most efficient of any other employee in the bureau, he received the highest service rating. 12.____

13. Only those members of the national organization who resided in the middle West attended the conference in Chicago. 13.____

14. The question of whether the office manager has as yet attained, or indeed can ever hope to secure professional status is one which has been discussed for years. 14.____

15. No one knew who to blame for the error which, we later discovered, resulted in a considerable loss of time. 15.____

KEY (CORRECT ANSWERS)

1.	A	6.	B	11.	D
2.	A	7.	A	12.	A
3.	B	8.	C	13.	C
4.	B	9.	A	14.	B
5.	D	10.	D	15.	A

TEST 2

DIRECTIONS: Each of the sentences in this test may be classified under one of the following four categories:

A. *Incorrect* because of faulty grammar or sentence structure
B. *Incorrect* because of faulty punctuation
C. *Incorrect* because of faulty capitalization
D. *Correct*

1. The National alliance of Businessmen is trying to persuade private businesses to hire youth in the summertime. 1.____

2. The supervisor who is on vacation, is in charge of processing vouchers. 2.____

3. The activity of the committee at its conferences is always stimulating. 3.____

4. After checking the addresses again, the letters went to the mailroom. 4.____

5. The director, as well as the employees, are interested in sharing the dividends. 5.____

KEY (CORRECT ANSWERS)

1. C
2. B
3. D
4. A
5. A

TEST 3

DIRECTIONS: In each of the following groups of sentences, one of the four sentences is faulty in grammar, punctuation, or capitalization. Select the INCORRECT sentence in each case.

1. A. Sailing down the bay was a thrilling experience for me. 1.____
   B. He was not consulted about your joining the club.
   C. This story is different than the one I told you yesterday.
   D. There is no doubt about his being the best player.

2. A. He maintains there is but one road to world peace. 2.____
   B. It is common knowledge that a child sees much he is not supposed to see.
   C. Much of the bitterness might have been avoided if arbitration had been resorted to earlier in the meeting.
   D. The man decided it would be advisable to marry a girl somewhat younger than him.

3. A. In this book, the incident I liked least is where the hero tries to put out the forest fire. 3.____
   B. Learning a foreign language will undoubtedly give a person a better understanding of his mother tongue.
   C. His actions made us wonder what he planned to do next.
   D. Because of the war, we were unable to travel during the summer vacation.

4. A. The class had no sooner become interested in the lesson than the dismissal bell rang. 4.____
   B. There is little agreement about the kind of world to be planned at the peace conference.
   C. "Today," said the teacher, "we shall read 'The Wind in the Willows,' I am sure you'll like it.
   D. The terms of the legal settlement of the family quarrel handicapped both sides for many years.

5. A. I was so surprised that I was not able to say a word. 5.____
   B. She is taller than any other member of the class.
   C. It would be much more preferable if you were never seen in his company.
   D. We had no choice but to excuse her for being late.

KEY (CORRECT ANSWERS)

1. C
2. D
3. A
4. C
5. C

TEST 4

DIRECTIONS: In each of the following groups of sentences, one of the four sentences is faulty in grammar, punctuation, or capitalization. Select the INCORRECT sentence in each case.

1. A. Please send me these data at the earliest opportunity. 1.____
   B. The loss of their material proved to be a severe handicap.
   C. My principal objection to this plan is that it is impracticable.
   D. The doll had laid in the rain for an hour and was ruined.

2. A. The garden scissors, left out all night in the rain, were in a badly rusted condition. 2.____
   B. The girls felt bad about the misunderstanding which had arisen
   C. Sitting near the campfire, the old man told John and I about many exciting adventures he had had.
   D. Neither of us is in a position to undertake a task of that magnitude.

3. A. The general concluded that one of the three roads would lead to the besieged city. 3.____
   B. The children didn't, as a rule, do hardly anything beyond what they were told to do.
   C. The reason the girl gave for her negligence was that she had acted on the spur of the moment.
   D. The daffodils and tulips look beautiful in that blue vase.

4. A. If I was ten years older, I should be interested in this work. 4.____
   B. Give the prize to whoever has drawn the best picture.
   C. When you have finished reading the book, take it back to the library.
   D. My drawing is as good as or better than yours.

5. A. He asked me whether the substance was animal or vegetable. 5.____
   B. An apple which is unripe should not be eaten by a child.
   C. That was an insult to me who am your friend.
   D. Some spy must of reported the matter to the enemy.

6. A. Limited time makes quoting the entire message impossible. 6.____
   B. Who did she say was going?
   C. The girls in your class have dressed more dolls this year than we.
   D. There was such a large amount of books on the floor that I couldn't find a place for my rocking chair.

7. A. What with his sleeplessness and his ill health, he was unable to assume any responsibility for the success of the meeting. 7.____
   B. If I had been born in February, I should be celebrating my birthday soon.
   C. In order to prevent breakage, she placed a sheet of paper between each of the plates when she packed them.
   D. After the spring shower, the violets smelled very sweet.

8. A. He had laid the book down very reluctantly before the end of the lesson. 8.____
   B. The dog, I am sorry to say, had lain on the bed all night.
   C. The cloth was first lain on a flat surface; then it was pressed with a hot iron.
   D. While we were in Florida, we lay in the sun until we were noticeably tanned.

9. A. If John was in New York during the recent holiday season, I have no doubt he spent most of the time with his parents. 9.____
   B. How could he enjoy the television program; the dog was barking and the baby was crying.
   C. When the problem was explained to the class, he must have been asleep.
   D. She wished that her new dress were finished so that she could go to the party.

10. A. The engine not only furnishes power but light and heat as well. 10.____
    B. You're aware that we've forgotten whose guilt was established, aren't you?
    C. Everybody knows that the woman made many sacrifices for her children.
    D. A man with his dog and gun is a familiar sight in this neighborhood.

KEY (CORRECT ANSWERS)

1.	D	6.	D
2.	C	7.	B
3.	B	8.	C
4.	A	9.	B
5.	D	10.	A

TEST 5

DIRECTIONS: Each of Questions 1 through 5 consists of a sentence which may be classified appropriately under one of the following four categories:

A. *Incorrect* because of faulty grammar
B. *Incorrect* because of faulty punctuation
C. *Incorrect* because of faulty spelling
D. *Correct*

Examine each sentence carefully. Then, print in the space at the right the letter preceding the category which is the BEST of the four suggested above

(Note: Each incorrect sentence contains only one type of error. Consider a sentence correct if it contains no errors, although there may be other correct ways of writing the sentence.)

1. Of the two employees, the one in our office is the most efficient. 1.____

2. No one can apply or even understand, the new rules and regulations. 2.____

3. A large amount of supplies were stored in the empty office. 3.____

4. If an employee is occassionally asked to work overtime, he should do so willingly. 4.____

5. It is true that the new procedures are difficult to use but, we are certain that you will learn them quickly. 5.____

6. The office manager said that he did not know who would be given a large allotment under the new plan. 6.____

7. It was at the supervisor's request that the clerk agreed to postpone his vacation. 7.____

8. We do not believe that it is necessary for both he and the clerk to attend the conference. 8.____

9. All employees, who display perseverance, will be given adequate recognition. 9.____

10. He regrets that some of us employees are dissatisfied with our new assignments. 10.____

11. "Do you think that the raise was merited," asked the supervisor? 11.____

12. The new manual of procedure is a valuable supplament to our rules and regulations. 12.____

13. The typist admitted that she had attempted to pursuade the other employees to assist her in her work. 13.____

14. The supervisor asked that all amendments to the regulations be handled by you and I. 14.____

15. The custodian seen the boy who broke the window. 15.____

KEY (CORRECT ANSWERS)

1.	A	6.	D	11.	B
2.	B	7.	D	12.	C
3.	A	8.	A	13.	C
4.	C	9.	B	14.	A
5.	B	10.	D	15.	A

INTERPRETING STATISTICAL DATA GRAPHS, CHARTS AND TABLES

EXAMINATION SECTION

TEST 1

DIRECTIONS: Each questioner incomplete statement is followed by several suggested answers or completions. Select the one that BEST answers the question or completes the statement. *PRINT THE LETTER OF THE CORRECT ANSWER IN THE SPACE AT THE RIGHT.*

Questions 1-3.

DIRECTIONS: Questions 1 through 3 are to be answered SOLELY on the basis of the following table.

QUARTERLY SALES REPORTED BY MAJOR INDUSTRY GROUPS

DECEMBER 2021 – FEBRUARY 2023

Reported Sales, Taxable & Non-Taxable (in Millions)

Industry Groups	12/21-2/22	3/22-5/22	6/22-8/22	9/22-11/22	12/22-2/23
Retailers	2,802	2,711	2,475	2,793	2,974
Wholesalers	2,404	2,237	2,269	2,485	2,974
Manufacturers	3,016	2,888	3,001	3,518	3,293
Services	1,034	1,065	984	1,132	1,092

1. The trend in total reported sales may be described as

   A. downward
   B. downward and upward
   C. horizontal
   D. upward

2. The two industry groups that reveal a similar seasonal pattern for the period December 2021 through November 2022 are

   A. retailers and manufacturers
   B. retailers and wholesalers
   C. wholesalers and manufacturers
   D. wholesalers and service

3. Reported sales were at a MINIMUM between

   A. December 2021 and February 2022
   B. March 2022 and May 2022
   C. June 2022 and August 2022
   D. September 2022 and November 2022

TEST 2

DIRECTIONS: Each question or incomplete statement is followed by several suggested answers or completions. Select the one that BEST answers the question or completes the statement. *PRINT THE LETTER OF THE CORRECT ANSWER IN THE SPACE AT THE RIGHT*

Questions 1-4.

DIRECTIONS: Questions 1 through 4 are to be answered SOLELY on the basis of the following information.

The income elasticity of demand for selected items of consumer demand in the United States are:

Item	Elasticity
Airline Travel	5.66
Alcohol	.62
Dentist Fees	1.00
Electric Utilities	3.00
Gasoline	1.29
Intercity Bus	1.89
Local Bus	1.41
Restaurant Meals	.75

1. The demand for the item listed below that would be MOST adversely affected by a decrease in income is

   A. alcohol
   B. electric utilities
   C. gasoline
   D. restaurant meals

2. The item whose relative change in demand would be the same as the relative change in income would be

   A. dentist fees
   B. gasoline
   C. restaurant meals
   D. none of the above

3. If income increases by 12 percent, the demand for restaurant meals may be expected to increase by

   A. 9 percent
   B. 12 percent
   C. 16 percent
   D. none of the above

4. On the basis of the above information, the item whose demand would be MOST adversely affected by an increase in the sales tax from 7 percent to 8 percent to be passed on to the consumer in the form of higher prices

   A. would be airline travel
   B. would be alcohol
   C. would be gasoline
   D. cannot be determined

TEST 3

DIRECTIONS: Each question or incomplete statement is followed by several suggested answers or completions. Select the one that BEST answers the question or completes the statement. *PRINT THE LETTER OF THE CORRECT ANSWER IN THE SPACE AT THE RIGHT.*

Questions 1-3.

DIRECTIONS: Questions 1 through 3 are to be answered SOLELY on the basis of the following graphs depicting various relationships in a single retail store.

GRAPH 1
RELATIONSHIP BETWEEN NUMBER OF CUSTOMERS
STORE AND TIME OF DAY

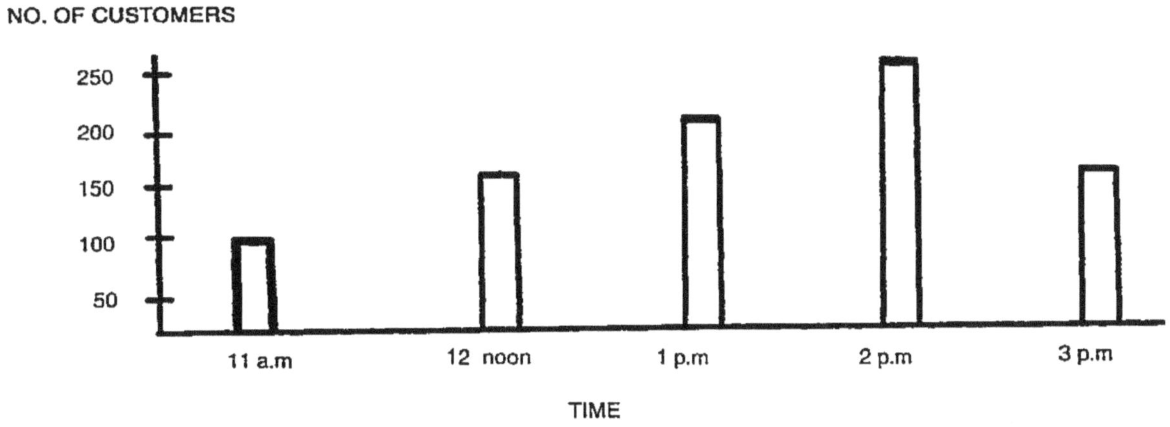

GRAPH II
RELATIONSHIP BETWEEN NUMBER OF CHECK-OUT LANES AVAILABLE IN STORE AND
WAIT TIME FOR CHECK-OUT

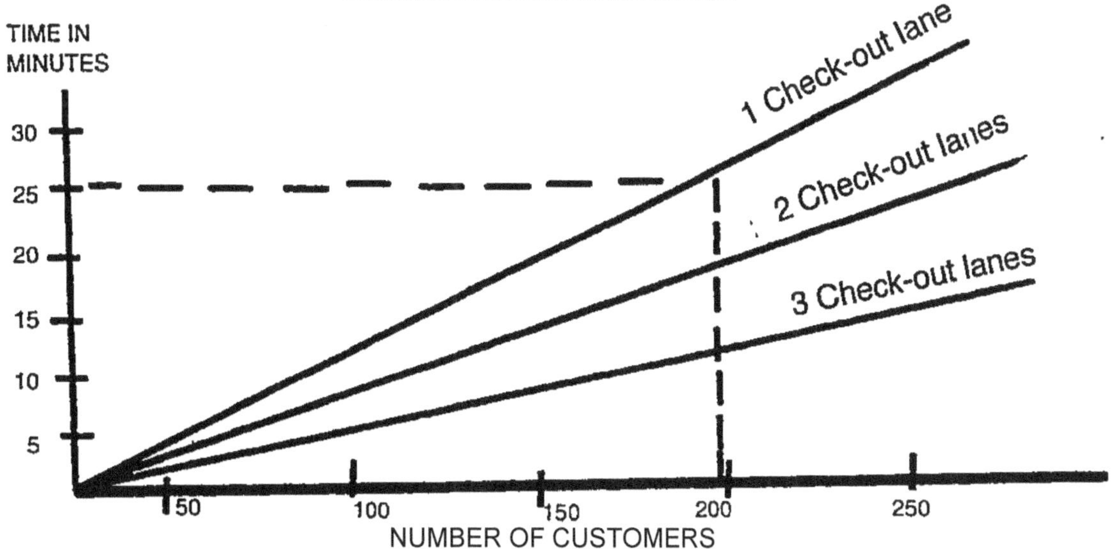

Note the dotted lines in Graph II. They demonstrate that, if there are 200 people in the store and only one check-out lane is open, the wait time will be 25 minutes.

1. At what time would a person be most likely NOT to have to wait more than 15 minutes if only one check-out lane is open?

   A. 11 A.M. B. 12 Noon C. 1 P.M. D. 3 P.M.

2. At what time of day would a person have to wait the LONGEST to check out if three check-out lanes are available?

   A. 11 A.M. B. 12 Noon C. 1 P.M. D. 2 P.M

3. The difference in wait times between 1 and 3 check-out lanes at 3 P.M. is MOST NEARLY

   A. 5 B. 10 C. 15 D. 20

TEST 4

DIRECTIONS: Each question or incomplete statement is followed by several suggested answers or completions. Select the one that BEST answers the question or completes the statement. *PRINT THE LETTER OF THE CORRECT ANSWER IN THE SPACE AT THE RIGHT.*

Questions 1-4.

DIRECTIONS: Questions 1 through 4 are to be answered SOLELY on the basis of the graph below.

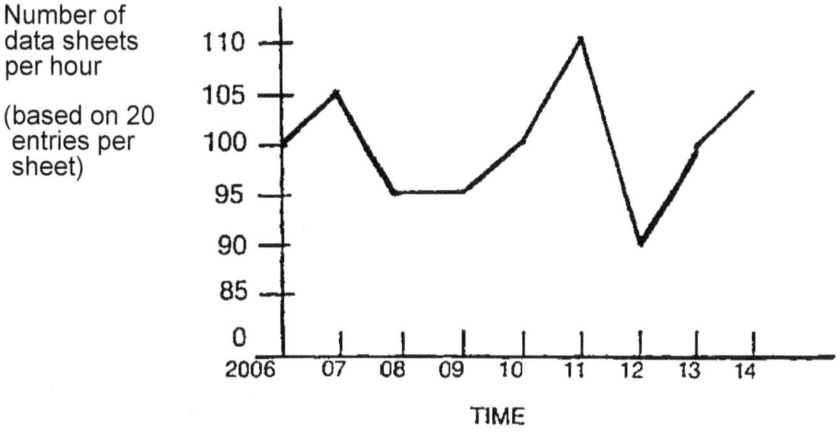

1. Of the following, during what four-year period did the average output of computer operators fall BELOW 100 sheets per hour?

   A. 2007-10 B. 2008-11 C. 2010-13 D. 2011-14

2. The average percentage change in output over the previous year's output for the years 2009 to 2012 is MOST NEARLY

   A. 2 B. 0 C. -5 D. -7

3. The difference between the actual output for 2012 and the projected figure based upon the average increase from 2006-2011 is MOST NEARLY

   A. 18 B. 20 C. 22 D. 24

4. Assume that after constructing the above graph you, an analyst, discovered that the average number of entries per sheet in 2012 was 25 (instead of 20) because of the complex nature of the work performed during that period.
   The average output in sheets per hour for the period 2010-13, expressed in terms of 20 items per sheet, would then be MOST NEARLY

   A. 95 B. 100 C. 105 D. 110

TEST 6

DIRECTIONS: Each question or incomplete statement is followed by several suggested answers or completions. Select the one that BEST answers the question or completes the statement. *PRINT THE LETTER OF THE CORRECT ANSWER IN THE SPACE AT THE RIGHT.*

Questions 1-3.

DIRECTIONS: Questions 1 through 3 are to be answered on the basis of the following data assembled for a cost-benefit analysis.

	Cost	Benefit
No program	0	0
Alternative W	$ 3,000	$ 6,000
Alternative X	$10,000	$17,000
Alternative Y	$17,000	$25,000
Alternative Z	$30,000	$32,000

1. From the point of view of selecting the alternative with the best cost benefit ratio, the BEST alternative is Alternative

   A. W   B. X   C. Y   D. Z

2. From the point of view of selecting the alternative with the best measure of net benefit, the BEST alternative is Alternative

   A. W   B. X   C. Y   D. Z

3. From the point of view of pushing public expenditure to the point where marginal benefit equals or exceeds marginal cost, the BEST alternative is Alternative

   A. W   B. X   C. Y   D. Z

TEST 6

DIRECTIONS: Each question or incomplete statement is followed by several suggested answers or completions. Select the one that BEST answers the question or completes the statement. *PRINT THE LETTER OF THE CORRECT ANSWER IN THE SPACE AT THE RIGHT.*

Questions 1-3.

DIRECTIONS: Questions 1 through 3 are to be answered SOLELY on the basis of the following data.

A series of cost-benefit studies of various alternative health programs yields the following results:

Program	Benefit	Cost
K	30	15
L	60	60
M	300	150
N	600	500

In answering Questions 1 and 2, assume that all programs can be increased or decreased in scale without affecting their individual benefit-to-cost ratios.

1. The benefit-to-cost ratio of Program M is

   A. 10:1 B. 5:1 C. 2:1 D. 1:2

2. The budget ceiling for one or more of the programs included in the study is set at 75 units. It may MOST logically be concluded that

   A. Programs K and L should be chosen to fit within the budget ceiling
   B. Program K would be the most desirable one that could be afforded
   C. Program M should be chosen rather than Program K
   D. the choice should be between Programs M and K

3. If no assumptions can be made regarding the effects of change of scale, the MOST logical conclusion, on the basis of the data available, is that

   A. more data are needed for a budget choice of program
   B. Program K is the most preferable because of its low cost and good benefit-to-cost ratio
   C. Program M is the most preferable because of its high benefits and good benefit-to-cost ratio
   D. there is no difference between Programs K and M, and either can be chosen for any purpose

TEST 7

DIRECTIONS: Each question or incomplete statement is followed by several suggested answers or completions. Select the one that BEST answers the question or completes the statement. *PRINT THE LETTER OF THE CORRECT ANSWER IN THE SPACE AT THE RIGHT.*

Questions 1-6.

DIRECTIONS: Questions 1 through 6 are to be answered SOLELY on the basis of the information contained in the charts below which relate to the budget allocations of City X, a small suburban community. The charts depict the annual budget allocations by Department and by expenditures over a five-year period.

CITY X BUDGET IN MILLIONS OF DOLLARS

TABLE I. Budget Allocations by Department

Department	2017	2018	2019	2020	2021
Public Safety	30	45	50	40	50
Health and Welfare	50	75	90	60	70
Engineering	5	8	10	5	8
Human Resources	10	12	20	10	22
Conservation & Environment	10	15	20	20	15
Education & Development	15	25	35	15	15
TOTAL BUDGET	120	180	225	150	180

TABLE II. Budget Allocations by Expenditures

Category	2017	2018	2019	2020	2021
Raw Materials & Machinery	36	63	68	30	98
Capital Outlay	12	27	56	15	18
Personal Services	72	90	101	105	64
TOTAL BUDGET	120	180	225	150	180

1. The year in which the SMALLEST percentage of the total annual budget was allocated to the Department of Education and Development is

   A. 2017 B. 2018 C. 2020 D. 2021

2. Assume that in 2020 the Department of Conservation and Environment divided its annual budget into the three categories of expenditures and in exactly the same proportion as the budget shown in Table II for the year 2020. The amount allocated for capital outlay in the Department of Conservation and Environment's 2020 budget was MOST NEARLY ______ million.

   A. $2 B. $4 C. $6 D. $10

3. From the year 2018 to the year 2020, the sum of the annual budgets for the Departments of Public Safety and Engineering showed an overall ______ million.

A. decline; SB
B. increase; $7
C. decline; S15
D. increase; S22

4. The LARGEST dollar increase in departmental budget allocations from one year to the next was in ______ from ______.

A. Public Safety; 2017 to 2018
B. Health and Welfare; 2017 to 2018
C. Education and Development; 2019 to 2020
D. Human Resources; 2019 to 2020

5. During the five-year period, the annual budget of the Department of Human Resources was GREATER than the annual budget for the Department of Conservation and Environment in ______ of the years.

A. none
B. one
C. two
D. three

6. If the total City X budget increases at the same rate from 2021 to 2022 as it did from 2020 to 2021, the total City X budget for 2022 will be MOST NEARLY ______ million.

A. $180
B. $200
C. $210
D. $215

TEST 8

DIRECTIONS: Each question or incomplete statement is followed by several suggested answers or completions. Select the one that BEST answers the question or completes the statement. *PRINT THE LETTER OF THE CORRECT ANSWER IN THE SPACE AT THE RIGHT.*

Questions 1-3.

DIRECTIONS: Questions 1 through 3 are to be answered SOLELY on the basis of the following information.

Assume that in order to encourage Program A, the State and Federal governments have agreed to make the following reimbursements for money spent on Program A, provided the unreimbursed balance is paid from City funds.

During Fiscal Year 2021-2022 - For the first $2 million expended, 50% Federal reimbursement and 30% State reimbursement; for the next $3 million, 40% Federal reimbursement and 20% State reimbursement; for the next $5 million, 20% Federal reimbursement and 10% State reimbursement. Above $10 million expended, no Federal or State reimbursement.

During Fiscal Year 2022-2023 - For the first $1 million expended, 30% Federal reimbursement and 20% State reimbursement; for the next $4 million, 15% Federal reimbursement and 10% State reimbursement. Above $5 million expended, no Federal or State reimbursement.

1. Assume that the Program A expenditures are such that the State reimbursement for Fiscal Year 2021-2022 will be $1 million.
   Then, the Federal reimbursement for Fiscal Year 2021-2022 will be

   A. $1,600,000 B. $1,800,000
   C. $2,000,000 D. $2,600,000

2. Assume that $8 million were to be spent on Program A in Fiscal Year 2022-2023.
   The TOTAL amount of unreimbursed City funds required would be

   A. $3,500,000 B. $4,500,000
   C. $5,500,000 D. $6,500,000

3. Assume that the City desires to have a combined total of $6 million spent in Program A during both the Fiscal Year 2021-2022 and the Fiscal Year 2022-2023.
   Of the following expenditure combinations, the one which results in the GREATEST reimbursement of City funds is ______ in Fiscal Year 2021-2022 and ______ in Fiscal Year 2022-2023.

   A. $5 million; $1 million B. $4 million; $2 million
   C. $3 million; $3 million D. $2 million; $4 million

KEY (CORRECT ANSWERS)

TEST 1

1. D
2. C
3. C

TEST 2

1. B
2. A
3. A
4. D

TEST 3

1. A
2. D
3. B

TEST 4

1. A
2. B
3. C
4. C

TEST 5

1. A
2. C
3. C

TEST 6

1. C
2. D
3. A

TEST 7

1. D
2. A
3. A
4. B
5. B
6. D

TEST 8

1. B
2. D
3. A

PHILOSOPHY, PRINCIPLES, PRACTICES, AND TECHNICS OF SUPERVISION, ADMINISTRATION, MANAGEMENT, AND ORGANIZATION

TABLE OF CONTENTS

PHILOSOPHY, PRINCIPLES, PRACTICES, AND TECHNICS
OF
SUPERVISION, ADMINISTRATION, MANAGEMENT, AND ORGANIZATION

MEANING OF SUPERVISION

The extension of the democratic philosophy has been accompanied by an extension in the scope of supervision. Modern leaders and supervisors no longer think of supervision in the narrow sense of being confined chiefly to visiting employees, supplying materials, or rating the staff. They regard supervision as being intimately related to all the concerned agencies of society, they speak of the supervisor's function in terms of "growth," rather than the "improvement" of employees.

This modern concept of supervision may be defined as follows: Supervision is leadership and the development of leadership within groups which are cooperatively engaged in inspection, research, training, guidance, and evaluation.

THE OLD AND THE NEW SUPERVISION

TRADITIONAL
1. Inspection
2. Focused on the employee
3. Visitation
4. Random and haphazard
5. Imposed and authoritarian
6. One person usually

MODERN
1. Study and analysis
2. Focused on aims, materials, methods, supervisors, employees, environment
3. Demonstrations, intervisitation, workshops, directed reading, bulletins, etc.
4. Definitely organized and planned (scientific)
5. Cooperative and democratic
6. Many persons involved (creative)

THE EIGHT (8) BASIC PRINCIPLES OF THE NEW SUPERVISION

I. Principle of Responsibility
Authority to act and responsibility for acting must be joined.
   A. If you give responsibility, give authority.
   B. Define employee duties clearly.
   C. Protect employees from criticism by others.
   D. Recognize the rights as well as obligations of employees.
   E. Achieve the aims of a democratic society insofar as it is possible within the area of your work.
   F. Establish a situation favorable to training and learning.
   G. Accept ultimate responsibility for everything done in your section, unit, office, division, department.
   H. Good administration and good supervision are inseparable.

II. Principle of Authority

The success of the supervisor is measured by the extent to which the power of authority is not used.

A. Exercise simplicity and informality in supervision
B. Use the simplest machinery of supervision
C. If it is good for the organization as a whole, it is probably justified.
D. Seldom be arbitrary or authoritative.
E. Do not base your work on the power of position or of personality.
F. Permit and encourage the free expression of opinions.

III. Principle of Self-Growth

The success of the supervisor is measured by the extent to which, and the speed with which, he is no longer needed.

A. Base criticism on principles, not on specifics.
B. Point out higher activities to employees.
C. Train for self-thinking by employees to meet new situations.
D. Stimulate initiative, self-reliance, and individual responsibility
E. Concentrate on stimulating the growth of employees rather than on removing defects.

IV. Principle of Individual Worth

Respect for the individual is a paramount consideration in supervision.

A. Be human and sympathetic in dealing with employees.
B. Don't nag about things to be done.
C. Recognize the individual differences among employees and seek opportunities to permit best expression of each personality.

V. Principle of Creative Leadership

The best supervision is that which is not apparent to the employee.

A. Stimulate, don't drive employees to creative action.
B. Emphasize doing good things.
C. Encourage employees to do what they do best.
D. Do not be too greatly concerned with details of subject or method.
E. Do not be concerned exclusively with immediate problems and activities.
F. Reveal higher activities and make them both desired and maximally possible.
G. Determine procedures in the light of each situation but see that these are derived from a sound basic philosophy.
H. Aid, inspire, and lead so as to liberate the creative spirit latent in all good employees.

VI. Principle of Success and Failure

There are no unsuccessful employees, only unsuccessful supervisors who have failed to give proper leadership.

A. Adapt suggestions to the capacities, attitudes, and prejudices of employees.
B. Be gradual, be progressive, be persistent.
C. Help the employee find the general principle; have the employee apply his own problem to the general principle.
D. Give adequate appreciation for good work and honest effort.
E. Anticipate employee difficulties and help to prevent them.
F. Encourage employees to do the desirable things they will do anyway.
G. Judge your supervision by the results it secures.

VII. Principle of Science
Successful supervision is scientific, objective, and experimental. It is based on facts, not on prejudices.
A. Be cumulative in results.
B. Never divorce your suggestions from the goals of training.
C. Don't be impatient of results.
D. Keep all matters on a professional, not a personal, level.
E. Do not be concerned exclusively with immediate problems and activities.
F. Use objective means of determining achievement and rating where possible.

VIII. Principle of Cooperation
Supervision is a cooperative enterprise between supervisor and employee.
A. Begin with conditions as they are.
B. Ask opinions of all involved when formulating policies.
C. Organization is as good as its weakest link.
D. Let employees help to determine policies and department programs.
E. Be approachable and accessible—physically and mentally.
F. Develop pleasant social relationships.

WHAT IS ADMINISTRATION

Administration is concerned with providing the environment, the material facilities, and the operational procedures that will promote the maximum growth and development of supervisors and employees. (Organization is an aspect and a concomitant of administration.)

There is no sharp line of demarcation between supervision and administration; these functions are intimately interrelated and, often, overlapping. They are complementary activities.

I. Practices Commonly Classed as "Supervisory"
A. Conducting employees' conferences
B. Visiting sections, units, offices, divisions, departments
C. Arranging for demonstrations
D. Examining plans
E. Suggesting professional reading
F. Interpreting bulletins
G. Recommending in-service training courses
H. Encouraging experimentation
I. Appraising employee morale
J. Providing for intervisitation

II. Practices Commonly Classified as "Administrative"
A. Management of the office
B. Arrangement of schedules for extra duties
C. Assignment of rooms or areas
D. Distribution of supplies
E. Keeping records and reports
F. Care of audio-visual materials
G. Keeping inventory records
H. Checking record cards and books

I. Programming special activities
J. Checking on the attendance and punctuality of employees

III. Practices Commonly Classified as Both "Supervisory" and "Administrative"
   A. Program construction
   B. Testing or evaluating outcomes
   C. Personnel accounting
   D. Ordering instructional materials

RESPONSIBILITIES OF THE SUPERVISOR

A person employed in a supervisory capacity must constantly be able to improve his own efficiency and ability. He represent the employer to the employees and only continuous self-examination can make him a capable supervisor.

Leadership and training are the supervisor's responsibility. An efficient working unit is one in which the employees work with the supervisor. It is his job to bring out the best in his employees. He must always be relaxed, courteous, and calm in his association with his employees. Their feelings are important, and a harsh attitude does not develop the most efficient employees.

COMPETENCES OF THE SUPERVISOR

I. Complete knowledge of the duties and responsibilities of his position.
II. To be able to organize a job, plan ahead, and carry through.
III. To have self-confidence and initiative.
IV. To be able to handle the unexpected situation and make quick decisions.
V. To be able to properly train subordinates in the positions they are best suited for.
VI. To be able to keep good human relations among his subordinates.
VII. To be able to keep good human relations between his subordinates and himself and to earn their respect and trust.

THE PROFESSIONAL SUPERVISOR-EMPLOYEE RELATIONSHIP

There are two kinds of efficiency: one kind is only apparent and is produced in organizations through the exercise of mere discipline; this is but a simulation of the second, or true, efficiency which springs from spontaneous cooperation. If you are a manager, no matter how great or small your responsibility, it is your job, in the final analysis, to create and develop this involuntary cooperation among the people whom you supervise. For, no matter how powerful a combination of money, machines, and materials a company may have, this is a dead and sterile thing without a team of willing, thinking, and articulate people to guide it.

The following 21 points are presented as indicative of the exemplary basic relationship that should exist between supervisor and employee:

1. Each person wants to be liked and respected by his fellow employee and wants to be treated with consideration and respect by his superior.
2. The most competent employee will make an error. However, in a unit where good relations exist between the supervisor and his employees, tenseness and fear do not exist. Thus, errors are not hidden or covered up, and the efficiency of a unit is not impaired.

3. Subordinates resent rules, regulations, or orders that are unreasonable or unexplained.
4. Subordinates are quick to resent unfairness, harshness, injustices, and favoritism.
5. An employee will accept responsibility if he knows that he will be complimented for a job well done, and not too harshly chastised for failure; that his supervisor will check the cause of the failure, and, if it was the supervisor's fault, he will assume the blame therefore. If it was the employee's fault, his supervisor will explain the correct method or means of handling the responsibility.
6. An employee wants to receive credit for a suggestion he has made, that is used. If a suggestion cannot be used, the employee is entitled to an explanation. The supervisor should not say "no" and close the subject.
7. Fear and worry slow up a worker's ability. Poor working environment can impair his physical and mental health. A good supervisor avoids forceful methods, threats, and arguments to get a job done.
8. A forceful supervisor is able to train his employees individually and as a team, and is able to motivate them in the proper channels.
9. A mature supervisor is able to properly evaluate his subordinates and to keep them happy and satisfied.
10. A sensitive supervisor will never patronize his subordinates.
11. A worthy supervisor will respect his employees' confidences.
12. Definite and clear-cut responsibilities should be assigned to each executive.
13. Responsibility should always be coupled with corresponding authority.
14. No change should be made in the scope or responsibilities of a position without a definite understanding to that effect on the part of all persons concerned.
15. No executive or employee, occupying a single position in the organization, should be subject to definite orders from more than one source.
16. Orders should never be given to subordinates over the head of a responsible executive. Rather than do this, the officer in question should be supplanted.
17. Criticisms of subordinates should, whoever possible, be made privately, and in no case should a subordinate be criticized in the presence of executives or employees of equal or lower rank.
18. No dispute or difference between executives or employees as to authority or responsibilities should be considered too trivial for prompt and careful adjudication.
19. Promotions, wage changes, and disciplinary action should always be approved by the executive immediately superior to the one directly responsible.
20. No executive or employee should ever be required, or expected, to be at the same time an assistant to, and critic of, another.
21. Any executive whose work is subject to regular inspection should, wherever practicable, be given the assistance and facilities necessary to enable him to maintain an independent check of the quality of his work.

MINI-TEXT IN SUPERVISION, ADMINISTRATION, MANAGEMENT, AND ORGANIZATION

I. Brief Highlights

Listed concisely and sequentially are major headings and important data in the field for quick recall and review.

A. Levels of Management

Any organization of some size has several levels of management. In terms of a ladder, the levels are:

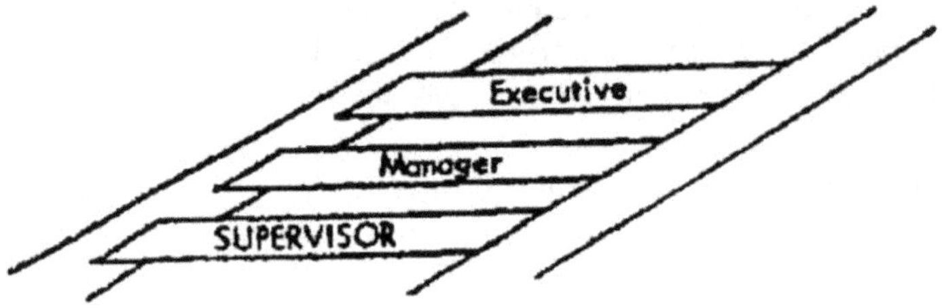

The first level is very important because it is the beginning point of management leadership.

B. What the Supervisor Must Learn

A supervisor must learn to:

1. Deal with people and their differences
2. Get the job done through people
3. Recognize the problems when they exist
4. Overcome obstacles to good performance
5. Evaluate the performance of people
6. Check his own performance in terms of accomplishment

C. A Definition of Supervisor

The term supervisor means any individual having authority, in the interests of the employer, to hire, transfer, suspend, lay-off, recall, promote, discharge, assign, reward, or discipline other employees or responsibility to direct them, or to adjust their grievances, or effectively to recommend such action, if, in connection with the foregoing, exercise of such authority is not of a merely routine or clerical nature but requires the use of independent judgment.

D. Elements of the Team Concept

What is involved in teamwork? The component parts are:

1. Members
2. A leader
3. Goals
4. Plans
5. Cooperation
6. Spirit

E. Principles of Organization

1. A team member must know what his job is.
2. Be sure that the nature and scope of a job are understood.
3. Authority and responsibility should be carefully spelled out.
4. A supervisor should be permitted to make the maximum number of decisions affecting his employees.
5. Employees should report to only one supervisor.
6. A supervisor should direct only as many employees as he can handle effectively.
7. An organization plan should be flexible.

8. Inspection and performance of work should be separate.
9. Organizational problems should receive immediate attention.
10. Assign work in line with ability and experience.

F. The Four Important Parts of Every Job

1. Inherent in every job is the *accountability* for results.
2. A second set of factors in every job is *responsibilities*.
3. Along with duties and responsibilities one must have the *authority* to act within certain limits without obtaining permission to proceed.
4. No job exists in a vacuum. The supervisor is surrounded by key *relationships*.

G. Principles of Delegation

Where work is delegated for the first time, the supervisor should think in terms of these questions:

1. Who is best qualified to do this?
2. Can an employee improve his abilities by doing this?
3. How long should an employee spend on this?
4. Are there any special problems for which he will need guidance?
5. How broad a delegation can I make?

H. Principles of Effective Communications

1. Determine the media.
2. To whom directed?
3. Identification and source authority.
4. Is communication understood?

I. Principles of Work Improvement

1. Most people usually do only the work which is assigned to them.
2. Workers are likely to fit assigned work into the time available to perform it.
3. A good workload usually stimulates output.
4. People usually do their best work when they know that results will be reviewed or inspected.
5. Employees usually feel that someone else is responsible for conditions of work, workplace layout, job methods, type of tools/equipment, and other such factors.
6. Employees are usually defensive about their job security.
7. Employees have natural resistance to change.
8. Employees can support or destroy a supervisor.
9. A supervisor usually earns the respect of his people through his personal example of diligence and efficiency.

J. Areas of Job Improvement

The areas of job improvement are quite numerous, but the most common ones which a supervisor can identify and utilize are:

1. Departmental layout
2. Flow of work
3. Workplace layout
4. Utilization of manpower
5. Work methods
6. Materials handling

7. Utilization
8. Motion economy

K. Seven Key Points in Making Improvements
1. Select the job to be improved
2. Study how it is being done now
3. Question the present method
4. Determine actions to be taken
5. Chart proposed method
6. Get approval and apply
7. Solicit worker participation

I. Corrective Techniques of Job Improvement
Specific Problems
1. Size of workload
2. Inability to meet schedules
3. Strain and fatigue
4. Improper use of men and skills
5. Waste, poor quality, unsafe conditions
6. Bottleneck conditions that hinder output
7. Poor utilization of equipment and machine
8. Efficiency and productivity of labor

General Improvement
1. Departmental layout
2. Flow of work
3. Work plan layout
4. Utilization of manpower
5. Work methods
6. Materials handling
7. Utilization of equipment
8. Motion economy

Corrective Techniques
1. Study with scale model
2. Flow chart study
3. Motion analysis
4. Comparison of units produced to standard allowance
5. Methods analysis
6. Flow chart and equipment study
7. Down time vs. running time
8. Motion analysis

M. A Planning Checklist
1. Objectives
2. Controls
3. Delegations
4. Communications
5. Resources
6. Manpower

7. Equipment
8. Supplies and materials
9. Utilization of time
10. Safety
11. Money
12. Work
13. Timing of improvements

N. Five Characteristics of Good Directions

In order to get results, directions must be:

1. Possible of accomplishment
2. Agreeable with worker interests
3. Related to mission
4. Planned and complete
5. Unmistakably clear

O. Types of Directions

1. Demands or direct orders
2. Requests
3. Suggestion or implication
4. volunteering

P. Controls

A typical listing of the overall areas in which the supervisor should establish controls might be:

1. Manpower
2. Materials
3. Quality of work
4. Quantity of work
5. Time
6. Space
7. Money
8. Methods

Q. Orienting the New Employee

1. Prepare for him
2. Welcome the new employee
3. Orientation for the job
4. Follow-up

R. Checklist for Orienting New Employees

	Yes	No
1. Do you appreciate the feelings of new employees when they first report for work?	___	___
2. Are you aware of the fact that the new employee must make a big adjustment to his job?	___	___
3. Have you given him good reasons for liking the job and the organization?	___	___
4. Have you prepared for his first day on the job?	___	___
5. Did you welcome him cordially and make him feel needed?	___	___

	Yes	No
6. Did you establish rapport with him so that he feels free to talk and discuss matters with you?	___	___
7. Did you explain his job to him and his relationship to you?	___	___
8. Does he know that his work will be evaluated periodically on a basis that is fair and objective?	___	___
9. Did you introduce him to his fellow workers in such a way that they are likely to accept him?	___	___
10. Does he know what employee benefits he will receive?	___	___
11. Does he understand the importance of being on the job and what to do if he must leave his duty station?	___	___
12. Has he been impressed with the importance of accident prevention and safe practice?	___	___
13. Does he generally know his way around the department?	___	___
14. Is he under the guidance of a sponsor who will teach the right way of doing things?	___	___
15. Do you plan to follow-up so that he will continue to adjust successfully to his job?	___	___

S. Principles of Learning
1. Motivation
2. Demonstration or explanation
3. Practice

T. Causes of Poor Performance
1. Improper training for job
2. Wrong tools
3. Inadequate directions
4. Lack of supervisory follow-up
5. Poor communications
6. Lack of standards of performance
7. Wrong work habits
8. Low morale
9. Other

U. Four Major Steps in On-The-Job Instruction
1. Prepare the worker
2. Present the operation
3. Tryout performance
4. Follow-up

V. Employees Want Five Things
1. Security
2. Opportunity
3. Recognition
4. Inclusion
5. Expression

W. Some Don'ts in Regard to Praise
1. Don't praise a person for something he hasn't done.
2. Don't praise a person unless you can be sincere.
3. Don't be sparing in praise just because your superior withholds it from you.
4. Don't let too much time elapse between good performance and recognition of it

X. How to Gain Your Workers' Confidence
Methods of developing confidence include such things as:
1. Knowing the interests, habits, hobbies of employees
2. Admitting your own inadequacies
3. Sharing and telling of confidence in others
4. Supporting people when they are in trouble
5. Delegating matters that can be well handled
6. Being frank and straightforward about problems and working conditions
7. Encouraging others to bring their problems to you
8. Taking action on problems which impede worker progress

Y. Sources of Employee Problems
On-the-job causes might be such things as:
1. A feeling that favoritism is exercised in assignments
2. Assignment of overtime
3. An undue amount of supervision
4. Changing methods or systems
5. Stealing of ideas or trade secrets
6. Lack of interest in job
7. Threat of reduction in force
8. Ignorance or lack of communications
9. Poor equipment
10. Lack of knowing how supervisor feels toward employee
11. Shift assignments

Off-the-job problems might have to do with:
1. Health
2. Finances
3. Housing
4. Family

Z. The Supervisor's Key to Discipline
There are several key points about discipline which the supervisor should keep in mind:
1. Job discipline is one of the disciplines of life and is directed by the supervisor.
2. It is more important to correct an employee fault than to fix blame for it.
3. Employee performance is affected by problems both on the job and off.
4. Sudden or abrupt changes in behavior can be indications of important employee problems.
5. Problems should be dealt with as soon as possible after they are identified.
6. The attitude of the supervisor may have more to do with solving problems than the techniques of problem solving.
7. Correction of employee behavior should be resorted to only after the supervisor is sure that training or counseling will not be helpful.

8. Be sure to document your disciplinary actions.
9. Make sure that you are disciplining on the basis of facts rather than personal feelings.
10. Take each disciplinary step in order, being careful not to make snap judgments, or decisions based on impatience.

AA. Five Important Processes of Management

1. Planning
2. Organizing
3. Scheduling
4. Controlling
5. Motivating

BB. When the Supervisor Fails to Plan

1. Supervisor creates impression of not knowing his job
2. May lead to excessive overtime
3. Job runs itself—supervisor lacks control
4. Deadlines and appointments missed
5. Parts of the work go undone
6. Work interrupted by emergencies
7. Sets a bad example
8. Uneven workload creates peaks and valleys
9. Too much time on minor details at expense of more important tasks

CC. Fourteen General Principles of Management

1. Division of work
2. Authority and responsibility
3. Discipline
4. Unity of command
5. Unity of direction
6. Subordination of individual interest to general interest
7. Remuneration of personnel
8. Centralization
9. Scalar chain
10. Order
11. Equity
12. Stability of tenure of personnel
13. Initiative
14. Esprit de corps

DD. Change

Bringing about change is perhaps attempted more often, and yet less well understood, than anything else the supervisor does. How do people generally react to change? (People tend to resist change that is imposed upon them by other individuals or circumstances.

Change is characteristic of every situation. It is a part of every real endeavor where the efforts of people are concerned.

1. Why do people resist change?
   People may resist change because of:
   a. Fear of the unknown
   b. Implied criticism
   c. Unpleasant experiences in the past
   d. Fear of loss of status
   e. Threat to the ego
   f. Fear of loss of economic stability

2. How can we best overcome the resistance to change?
   In initiating change, take these steps:
   a. Get ready to sell
   b. Identify sources of help
   c. Anticipate objections
   d. Sell benefits
   e. Listen in depth
   f. Follow up

II. Brief Topical Summaries

A. Who/What is the Supervisor?
   1. The supervisor is often called the "highest level employee and the lowest level manager."
   2. A supervisor is a member of both management and the work group. He acts as a bridge between the two.
   3. Most problems in supervision are in the area of human relations, or people problems.
   4. Employees expect: Respect, opportunity to learn and to advance, and a sense of belonging, and so forth.
   5. Supervisors are responsible for directing people and organizing work. Planning is of paramount importance.
   6. A position description is a set of duties and responsibilities inherent to a given position.
   7. It is important to keep the position description up-to-date and to provide each employee with his own copy.

B. The Sociology of Work
   1. People are alike in many ways; however, each individual is unique.
   2. The supervisor is challenged in getting to know employee differences. Acquiring skills in evaluating individuals is an asset.
   3. Maintaining meaningful working relationships in the organization is of great importance.
   4. The supervisor has an obligation to help individuals to develop to their fullest potential.
   5. Job rotation on a planned basis helps to build versatility and to maintain interest and enthusiasm in work groups.
   6. Cross training (job rotation) provides backup skills.

7. The supervisor can help reduce tension by maintaining a sense of humor, providing guidance to employees, and by making reasonable and timely decisions. Employees respond favorably to working under reasonably predictable circumstances.
8. Change is characteristic of all managerial behavior. The supervisor must adjust to changes in procedures, new methods, technological changes, and to a number of new and sometimes challenging situations.
9. To overcome the natural tendency for people to resist change, the supervisor should become more skillful in initiating change.

C. Principles and Practices of Supervision

1. Employees should be required to answer to only one superior.
2. A supervisor can effectively direct only a limited number of employees, depending upon the complexity, variety, and proximity of the jobs involved.
3. The organizational chart presents the organization in graphic form. It reflects lines of authority and responsibility as well as interrelationships of units within the organization.
4. Distribution of work can be improved through an analysis using the "Work Distribution Chart."
5. The "Work Distribution Chart" reflects the division of work within a unit in understandable form.
6. When related tasks are given to an employee, he has a better chance of increasing his skills through training.
7. The individual who is given the responsibility for tasks must also be given the appropriate authority to insure adequate results.
8. The supervisor should delegate repetitive, routine work. Preparation of recurring reports, maintaining leave and attendance records are some examples.
9. Good discipline is essential to good task performance. Discipline is reflected in the actions of employees on the job in the absence of supervision.
10. Disciplinary action may have to be taken when the positive aspects of discipline have failed. Reprimand, warning, and suspension are examples of disciplinary action.
11. If a situation calls for a reprimand, be sure it is deserved and remember it is to be done in private.

D. Dynamic Leadership

1. A style is a personal method or manner of exerting influence.
2. Authoritarian leaders often see themselves as the source of power and authority.
3. The democratic leader often perceives the group as the source of authority and power.
4. Supervisors tend to do better when using the pattern of leadership that is most natural for them.
5. Social scientists suggest that the effective supervisor use the leadership style that best fits the problem or circumstances involved.
6. All four styles—telling, selling, consulting, joining—have their place. Using one does not preclude using the other at another time.

7. The theory X point of view assumes that the average person dislikes work, will avoid it whenever possible, and must be coerced to achieve organizational objectives.
8. The theory Y point of view assumes that the average person considers work to be a natural as play, and, when the individual is committed, he requires little supervision or direction to accomplish desired objectives.
9. The leader's basic assumptions concerning human behavior and human nature affect his actions, decisions, and other managerial practices.
10. Dissatisfaction among employees is often present, but difficult to isolate. The supervisor should seek to weaken dissatisfaction by keeping promises, being sincere and considerate, keeping employees informed, and so forth.
11. Constructive suggestions should be encouraged during the natural progress of the work.

E. Processes for Solving Problems
1. People find their daily tasks more meaningful and satisfying when they can improve them.
2. The causes of problems, or the key factors, are often hidden in the background. Ability to solve problems often involves the ability to isolate them from their backgrounds. There is some substance to the cliché that some persons "can't see the forest for the trees."
3. New procedures are often developed from old ones. Problems should be broken down into manageable parts. New ideas can be adapted from old one.
4. People think differently in problem-solving situations. Using a logical, patterned approach is often useful. One approach found to be useful includes these steps:
    a. Define the problem
    b. Establish objectives
    c. Get the facts
    d. Weigh and decide
    e. Take action
    f. Evaluate action

F. Training for Results
1. Participants respond best when they feel training is important to them.
2. The supervisor has responsibility for the training and development of those who report to him.
3. When training is delegated to others, great care must be exercised to insure the trainer has knowledge, aptitude, and interest for his work as a trainer.
4. Training (learning) of some type goes on continually. The most successful supervisor makes certain the learning contributes in a productive manner to operational goals.
5. New employees are particularly susceptible to training. Older employees facing new job situations require specific training, as well as having need for development and growth opportunities.
6. Training needs require continuous monitoring.
7. The training officer of an agency is a professional with a responsibility to assist supervisors in solving training problems.

8. Many of the self-development steps important to the supervisor's own growth are equally important to the development of peers and subordinates. Knowledge of these is important when the supervisor consults with others on development and growth opportunities.

G. Health, Safety, and Accident Prevention

1. Management-minded supervisors take appropriate measures to assist employees in maintaining health and in assuring safe practices in the work environment.
2. Effective safety training and practices help to avoid injury and accidents.
3. Safety should be a management goal. All infractions of safety which are observed should be corrected without exception.
4. Employees' safety attitude, training and instruction, provision of safe tools and equipment, supervision, and leadership are considered highly important factors which contribute to safety and which can be influenced directly by supervisors.
5. When accidents do occur, they should be investigated promptly for very important reasons, including the fact that information which is gained can be used to prevent accidents in the future.

H. Equal Employment Opportunity

1. The supervisor should endeavor to treat all employees fairly, without regard to religion, race, sex, or national origin.
2. Groups tend to reflect the attitude of the leader. Prejudice can be detected even in very subtle form. Supervisors must strive to create a feeling of mutual respect and confidence in every employee.
3. Complete utilization of all human resources is a national goal. Equitable consideration should be accorded women in the work force, minority-group members, the physically and mentally handicapped, and the older employee. The important question is: "Who can do the job?"
4. Training opportunities, recognition for performance, overtime assignments, promotional opportunities, and all other personnel actions are to be handled on an equitable basis.

I. Improving Communications

1. Communications is achieving understanding between the sender and the receiver of a message. It also means sharing information—the creation of understanding.
2. Communication is basic to all human activity. Words are means of conveying meanings; however, real meanings are in people.
3. There are very practical differences in the effectiveness of one-way, impersonal, and two-way communications. Words spoken face-to-face are better understood. Telephone conversations are effective, but lack the rapport of person-to-person exchanges. The whole person communicates.
4. Cooperation and communication in an organization go hand in hand. When there is a mutual respect between people, spelling out rules and procedures for communicating is unnecessary.
5. There are several barriers to effective communications. These include failure to listen with respect and understanding, lack of skill in feedback, and misinterpreting the meanings of words used by the speaker. It is also common

practice to listen to what we want to hear, and tune out things we do not want to hear.

6. Communication is management's chief problem. The supervisor should accept the challenge to communicate more effectively and to improve interagency and intra-agency communications.
7. The supervisor may often plan for and conduct meetings. The planning phase is critical and may determine the success or the failure of a meeting.
8. Speaking before groups usually requires extra effort. Stage fright may never disappear completely, but it can be controlled.

J. Self-Development

1. Every employee is responsible for his own self-development.
2. Toastmaster and toastmistress clubs offer opportunities to improve skills in oral communications.
3. Planning for one's own self-development is of vital importance. Supervisors know their own strengths and limitations better than anyone else.
4. Many opportunities are open to aid the supervisor in his developmental efforts, including job assignments; training opportunities, both governmental and non-governmental—to include universities and professional conferences and seminars.
5. Programmed instruction offers a means of studying at one's own rate.
6. Where difficulties may arise from a supervisor's being away from his work for training, he may participate in televised home study or correspondence courses to meet his self-development needs.

K. Teaching and Training

1. The Teaching Process

   Teaching is encouraging and guiding the learning activities of students toward established goals. In most cases this process consists of five steps: preparation, presentation, summarization, evaluation, and application.

   a. Preparation

      Preparation is two-fold in nature; that of the supervisor and the employee. Preparation by the supervisor is absolutely essential to success. He must know what, when, where, how, and whom he will teach. Some of the factors that should be considered are:

      1) The objectives
      2) The materials needed
      3) The methods to be used
      4) Employee participation
      5) Employee interest
      6) Training aids
      7) Evaluation
      8) Summarization

      Employee preparation consists in preparing the employee to receive the material. Probably the most important single factor in the preparation of the employee is arousing and maintaining his interest. He must know the objectives of the training, why he is there, how the material can be used, and its importance to him.

b. Presentation
In presentation, have a carefully designed plan and follow it. The plan should be accurate and complete, yet flexible enough to meet situations as they arise. The method of presentation will be determined by the particular situation and objectives.

c. Summary
A summary should be made at the end of every training unit and program. In addition, there may be internal summaries depending on the nature of the material being taught. The important thing is that the trainee must always be able to understand how each part of the new material relates to the whole.

d. Application
The supervisor must arrange work so the employee will be given a chance to apply new knowledge or skills while the material is still clear in his mind and interest is high. The trainee does not really know whether he has learned the material until he has been given a chance to apply it. If the material is not applied, it loses most of its value.

e. Evaluation
The purpose of all training is to promote learning. To determine whether the training has been a success or failure, the supervisor must evaluate this learning.
In the broadest sense, evaluation includes all the devices, methods, skills, and techniques used by the supervisor to keep himself and the employees informed as to their progress toward the objectives they are pursuing. The extent to which the employee has mastered the knowledge, skills, and abilities, or changed his attitudes, as determined by the program objectives, is the extent to which instruction has succeeded or failed.
Evaluation should not be confined to the end of the lesson, day, or program but should be used continuously. We shall note later the way this relates to the rest of the teaching process.

2. Teaching Methods
A teaching method is a pattern of identifiable student and instructor activity used in presenting training material.
All supervisors are faced with the problem of deciding which method should be used at a given time.

a. Lecture
The lecture is direct oral presentation of material by the supervisor. The present trend is to place less emphasis on the trainer's activity and more on that of the trainee.

b. Discussion
Teaching by discussion or conference involves using questions and other techniques to arouse interest and focus attention upon certain areas, and by doing so creating a learning situation. This can be one of the most

valuable methods because it gives the employees an opportunity to express their ideas and pool their knowledge.

c. Demonstration
The demonstration is used to teach how something works or how to do something. It can be used to show a principle or what the results of a series of actions will be. A well-staged demonstration is particularly effective because it shows proper methods of performance in a realistic manner.

d. Performance
Performance is one of the most fundamental of all learning techniques or teaching methods. The trainee may be able to tell how a specific operation should be performed but he cannot be sure he knows how to perform the operation until he has done so.
As with all methods, there are certain advantages and disadvantages to each method.

e. Which Method to Use
Moreover, there are other methods and techniques of teaching. It is difficult to use any method without other methods entering into it. In any learning situation, a combination of methods is usually more effective than any one method alone.

Finally, evaluation must be integrated into the other aspects of the teaching-learning process.

It must be used in the motivation of the trainees; it must be used to assist in developing understanding during the training; and it must be related to employee application of the results of training.

This is distinctly the role of the supervisor.

BASIC FUNDAMENTALS OF A FINANCIAL STATEMENT

TABLE OF CONTENTS

BASIC FUNDAMENTALS OF A FINANCIAL STATEMENT

COMMENTARY

The ability to read and understand a financial statement is a basic requirement for the accountant, auditor, account clerk, bookkeeper, bank examiner, budget examiner, and, of course, for the executive who must manage and administer departmental affairs.

FINANCIAL REPORTS

Are financial reports really as difficult as all that? Well, if you know they are not so difficult because you have worked with them before, this section will be of auxiliary help for you. However, if you find financial statements a bit murky, but realize their great importance to you, we ought to get along fine together. For "mathematics," all we'll use is fourth-grade arithmetic.

Accountants, like all other professionals, have developed a specialized vocabulary. Sometimes this is helpful and sometimes plain confusing (like their practice of calling the income account, "Statement of Profit and Loss," when it is bound to be one or the other). But there are really only a score or so technical terms that you will have to get straight in mind. After that is done, the whole foggy business will begin to clear and in no time at all you'll be able to talk as wisely as the next fellow.

BALANCE SHEET

Look at the sample balance sheet printed on Page 2, and we'll have an insight into how it is put together. This particular report is neither the simplest that could be issued, nor the most complicated. It is a good average sample of the kind of report issues by an up-to-date manufacturing company.

Note particularly that the balance sheet represents the situation as it stood on one particular day, December 31, not the record of a year's operation. This balance sheet is broken into two parts on the left are shown *ASSETS* and on the right *LIABILITIES*. Under the asset column, you will find listed the value of things the company owns or are owed to the company. Under liabilities are listed the things the company owes to others, plus reserves, surplus, and the stated value of the stockholders' interest in the company.

One frequently hears the comment, "Well, I don't see what a good balance sheet is anyway, because the assets and liabilities are always the same whether the company is successful or not."

It is true that they always balance and, by itself, a balance sheet doesn't tell much until it is analyzed. Fortunately, we can make a balance sheet tell its story without too much effort–often an extremely revealing story, particularly, if we compare the records of several years.

ASSETS

The first notation on the asset side of the balance sheet is *CURRENT ASSETS* (Item 1). In general, current assets include cash and things that can be turned into cash in a hurry, or that, in the normal course of business, will be turned into cash in the reasonably near future, usually within a year.

Item 2 on our sample sheet is *CASH*. Cash is just what you would expect–bills and silver in the till and money on deposit in the bank.

UNITED STATES GOVERNMENT SECURITIES is Item 3. The general practice is to show securities listed as current assets at cost or market value, whichever is lower. The figure, for all reasonable purposes, represents the amount by which total cash could be easily increased if the company wanted to sell these securities.

The next entry is *ACCOUNTS RECEIVABLE* (Item 4). Here we find the total amount of money owed to the company by its regular business creditors and collectable within the next year. Most of the money is owed to the company by its customers for goods that the company delivered on credit. If this were a department store instead of a manufacturer, what you owed the store on our charge account would be included here. Because some people fail to pay their bills, the company sets up a reserve for doubtful accounts, which it subtracts from all the money owed.

THE ABC MANUFACTURING COMPANY, INC.
CONSOLIDATED BALANCE SHEET – DECEMBER 31

Item			Item		
1. CURRENT ASSETS			16. CURRENT LIABILITIES		
2. Cash			17. Accts. Payable		$300,00
3. U.S. Government Securities			18. Accrued Taxes		800,00
4. Accounts Receivable		2,000,000	19. Accrued Wages, interest		
(less reserves)			and Other Expenses		370,00
5. Inventories (at lower of cost or			20. Total Current Liabilities		$1,470,00
market)		2,000,000	21. FIRST MORTGAGE SINK-		
6. Total Current Assets		$7,000,000	ING FUND BONDS, 3½ %		
7. INVESTMENT IN AFFILIATED			DUE 2020		$2,000,00
COMPANY			22. RESERVE FOR		
Not consolidated (at cost, not in			CONTINGENCIES		200,00
excess of net assets)		200,000	23. CAPITAL STOCK:		
8. OTHER INVESTMENTS			24. 5% Preferred Stock		
At cost, less than market		100,000	(authorized and issued		
9. PLANT IMPROVEMENT FUND		550,000	10,000 shares of $100 par		
10. PROPERTY, PLANT AND			shares of $100		
EQUIPMENT:			(par value)	$1,000,000	
Cost	$8,000,000		25. Common stock		
11. Less Reserve			(authorized and issued		
for Depreciation	5,000,000		400,000 shares of no		
12. NET PROPERTY		3,000,000	par value)	1,000,000	
13. PREPAYMENTS		50,000	26. SURPLUS:		2,000,00
14. DEFERRED CHARGES		100,000	27. Earned	3,530,000	
15. PATENTS AND GOODWILL		100,000	28. Capital (arising from sale		
			of common capital stock		
			at price in excess of		
			stated value)	1,900,000	
					5,430,00
TOTAL		$11,000,000	TOTAL		$11,100,00

Item 5, *INVENTORIES*, is the value the company places on the supplies it owns. The inventory of a manufacturer may contain raw materials that it uses in making the things it sells, partially finished goods in process of manufacture, and, finally, completed merchandise that it is ready to sell. Several methods are used to arrive at the value placed on these various items. The most common is to value them at their cost or present market value, whichever is lower.

You can be reasonably confident, however, that the figure given is an honest and significant one for the particular industry if the report is certified by a reputable firm of public accountants.

Next on the asset side is *TOTAL CURRENT ASSETS* (Item 6). This is an extremely important figure when used in connection with other items in the report, which we will come to presently. Then we will discover how to make total current assets tell their story.

INVESTMENT IN AFFILIATED COMPANY Item 7) represents the cost to our parent company of the capital stock of its subsidiary or affiliated company. A subsidiary is simply one company that is controlled by another. Most corporations that own other companies outright lump the figures in a CONSOLIDATED BALANCE SHEET. This means that, under cash, for example, one would find a total figure that represented all of the cash of the parent company and of its wholly owned subsidiary. This is a perfectly reasonable procedure because, in the last analysis, all of the money is controlled by the same persons.

Our typical company shows that it has *OTHER INVESTMENTS* (Item 8), in addition to its affiliated company. Sometimes good marketable securities other than Government bonds are carried as current assets, but the more conservative practice is to list these other security holdings separately. If they have been bought as a permanent investment, they would always be shown by themselves. "At cost, less than market" means that our company paid $100,000 for these other investments, but they are now worth more.

Among our assets is a *PLANT IMPROVEMENT FUND* (Item 9). Of course, this item does not appear in all company balance sheets, but is typical of special funds that companies set up for one purpose or another. For example, money set aside to pay off part of the bonded debt of a company might be segregated into a special fund. The money our directors have put aside to improve the plant would often be invested in Government bonds,

FIXED ASSETS

The next item (10) is *PROPERTY, PLANT, AND EQUIPMENT*, but it might just as well be labeled Fixed Assets as these items are used more or less interchangeably, Under Item 10, the report gives the value of land, buildings, and machinery and such movable things as trucks, furniture, and hand tools. Historically, probably more sins were committed against this balance sheet item than any other.

In olden days, cattlemen used to drive their stock to market in the city. It was a common trick to stop outside of town, spread out some salt for the cattle to make them thirsty and then let them drink all the water they could hold. When they were weighed for sale, the cattlemen would collect cash for the water the stock had drunk. Business buccaneers, taking the cue from their farmer friends, would often "write up" the value of their fixed assets. In other words, they would increase the value shown on the balance sheet, making the capital stock appear to be worth a lot more than it was. *Watered stock* proved a bad investment for most stockholders. The practice has, fortunately, been stopped, though it took major financial reorganizations to squeeze the water out of some securities.

The most common practice today is to list fixed assets at cost. Often, there is no ready market for most of the things that fall under this heading, so it is not possible to give market value. A good report will tell what is included under fixed assets and how it has been valued. If the value has been increased by *write-up* or decreased by *write-down*, a footnote explanation is usually given. A *write-up* might occur, for instance, if the value of real estate increased substantially. A *write-down* might follow the invention of a new machine that put an important part of the company's equipment out of date.

DEPRECIATION

Naturally, all of the fixed property of a company will wear out in time (except, of course, non-agricultural land). In recognition of this fact, companies set up a *RESERVE FOR APPRECIATION* (Item 11). If a truck costs $4,000 and is expected to last four years, it will be depreciated at the rate of $1,000 a year.

Two other items also frequently occur in connection with depreciation–*depletion* and *obsolescence.* Companies may lump depreciation, depletion, and obsolescence under a single title, or list them separately.

Depletion is a term used primarily by mining and oil companies (or any of the so-called extractive industries). Depletion means exhaust or use up. As the oil or other natural resource is used up, a reserve is set up, to compensate for the natural wealth the company no longer owns. This reserve is set up in recognition of the fact that, as the company sells its natural product, it must get back not only the cost of extracting but also the original cost of the natural resource.

Obsolescence represents the loss in value because a piece of property has gone out of date before it wore out. Airplanes are modern examples of assets that tend to get behind the times long before the parts wear out. (Women and husbands will be familiar with the speed at which ladies' hats "obsolesce.")

In our sample balance sheet we have placed the reserve for depreciation under fixed assets and then subtracted, giving us *NET PROPERTY* (Item 12), which we add into the asset column. Sometimes, companies put the reserve for depreciation in the liability column. As you can see, the effect is just the same whether it is *subtracted* from assets or *added* to liabilities.

The manufacturer, whose balance sheet we use, rents a New York showroom and pays his rent yearly, in advance. Consequently, he has listed under assets *PREPAYMENTS* (Item 13). This is listed as an asset because he has paid for the use of the showroom, but has not yet received the benefit from its use. The use is something coming to the firm in the following year and, hence, is an asset. The dollar value of this asset will decrease by one-twelfth each month during the coming year.

DEFERRED CHARGES (Item 14) represents a type of expenditure similar to prepayment. For example, our manufacturer brought out a new product last year, spending $100,000 introducing it to the market. As the benefit from this expenditure will be returned over months or even years to come, the manufacturer did not think it reasonable to charge the full expenditure against costs during the year. He has *deferred* the charges and will write them off gradually.

INTANGIBLES

The last entry in our asset column is *PATENTS AND GOODWILL* (Item 15). If our company were a young one, set up to manufacturer some new patented product, it would probably carry its patents at a substantial figure. In fact, *intangibles* of both old and new companies are often of great but generally unmeasurable worth.

Company practice varies considerably in assigning value to intangibles. Proctor & Gamble, despite the tremendous goodwill that has been built up for *Ivory Soap*, has reduced all of its intangibles to the nominal $1. Some of the big cigarette companies, on the contrary, place a high dollar value on the goodwill their brand names enjoy. Companies that spend a good deal for research and the development of new products are more inclined than others to reflect this fact in the value assigned to patents, license agreements, etc.

LIABILITIES

The liability side of the balance sheet appears a little deceptive at first glance. Several of the entries simply don't sound like liabilities by any ordinary definition of the term.

The first term on the liability side of any balance sheet is usually *CURRENT LIABILITIES* (Item 16). This is a companion to the Current Assets item across the page and includes all debts that fall due within the next year. The relation between current assets and current liabilities is one of the most revealing things to be gotten from the balance sheet, but we will go into that quite thoroughly later on.

ACCOUNTS PAYABLE (Item 17) represents the money that the company owes to its ordinary business creditors–unpaid bills for materials, supplies, insurance, and the like. Many companies itemize the money they owe in a much more detailed fashion than we have done, but, as you will see, the totals are the most interesting thing to us.

Item 18, *ACCRUED TAXES*, is the tax bill that the company estimates it still owes for the past year. We have lumped all taxes in our balance sheet, as many companies do. However, sometimes you will find each type of tax given separately. If the detailed procedure is followed, the description of the tax is usually quite sufficient to identify the separate items.

Accounts Payable was defined as the money the company owed to its regular business creditors. The company also owes, on any given day, wages to its own employees; interest to its bondholders and to banks from which it may have borrowed money; fees to its attorneys; pensions, etc. These are all totaled under *ACCRUED WAGES, INTEREST AND OTHER EXPENSES* (Item 19).

TOTAL CURRENT LIABILITIES (Item 20) is just the sum of everything that the company owed on December 31 and which must be paid sometime in the next twelve months.

It is quite clear that all of the things discussed above are liabilities. The rest of the entries on the liability side of the balance sheet, however, do not seem at first glance to be liabilities.

Our balance sheet shows that the company, on December 31, had $2,000,000 of 3½ percent First Mortgage BONDS outstanding (Item 21). Legally, the money received by a company when it sells bonds is considered a loan to the company. Therefore, it is obvious that the company owes to the bondholders an amount equal to the face value or the *call price* of the bonds it has outstanding. The call price is a figure usually larger than the face value of the bonds at which price the company can *call* the bonds in from the bondholders and pay them off before they ordinarily fall due. The date that often occurs as part of the name of a bond is the date at which the company has promised to pay off the loan from the bondholders.

RESERVES

The next heading, *RESERVE FOR CONTINGENCIES* (Item 22) sounds more like an asset than a liability. "My reserves," you might say, "are dollars in the bank, and dollars in the bank are assets.

No one would deny that you have something there. In fact, the corporation treasurer also has his reserve for contingencies balanced by either cash or some kind of unspecified investment on the asset side of the ledger. His reason for setting up a reserve on the liability side of the balance sheet is a precaution against making his financial position seem better than it is. He decided that the company might have to pay out this money during the coming year if certain things happened. If he did not set up the "reserve," his surplus would appear larger by an amount equal to his reserve.

A very large reserve for contingencies or a sharp increase in this figure from the previous year should be examined closely by the investor. Often, in the past, companies tried to hide their true earnings by transferring funds into a contingency reserve. As a reserve looks somewhat like a true liability, stockholders were confused about the real value of their securities. When a reserve is not set up for protection against some very probable loss or expenditure, it should be considered by the investor as part of surplus.

CAPITAL STOCK

Below reserves there is a major heading, *CAPITAL STOCK* (Item 23). Companies may have one type of security outstanding, or they may have a dozen. All of the issues that represent shares of ownership are capital, regardless of what they are called on the balance sheet—preferred stock, preference stock, common stock, founders' shares, capital stock, or something else.

Our typical company has one issue of 5 percent *PREFERRED STOCK* (Item 24). It is called *preferred* because those who own it have a right to dividends and assets before the *common* stockholders—that is, the holders are in a preferred position as owners. Usually, preferred stockholders do not have a voice in company affairs unless the company fails to pay them dividends at the promised rate. Their rights to dividends are almost always *cumulative.* This simply means that all past dividends must be paid before the other stockholders can receive anything. Preferred stockholders are not creditors of the company so it cannot properly be said that the company *owes* them the value of their holdings. However, in case the company decided to go out of business, preferred stockholders would have a prior claim on anything that was left in the company treasury after all of the creditors, including the bondholders, were paid off. In practice, this right does not always mean much, but it does explain why the book value of their holdings is carried as a liability.

COMMON STOCK (Item 25) is simple enough as far as definition is concerned. It represents the rights of the ordinary owner of the company. Each company has as many owners as it has stockholders. The proportion of the company that each stockholder owns is determined by the number of shares he has. However, neither the book value of a no-par common stock, nor the par value of an issue that has a given par, can be considered as representing either the original sale price, the market value, or what would be left for the stockholders if the company were liquidated.

A profitable company will seldom be dissolved. Once things have taken such a turn that dissolution appears desirable, the stated value of the stock is generally nothing but a fiction. Even if the company is profitable as a going institution, once it ceases to function even its tangible assets drop in value because there is not usually a ready market for its inventory of raw materials and semi-finished goods, or its plant and machinery.

SURPLUS

The last major heading on the liability side of the balance sheet is *SURPLUS* (Item 26). The surplus, of course, is not a liability in the popular sense at all. It represents, on our balance sheet, the difference between the stated value of our common stock and the net assets behind the stock.

Two different kinds of surplus frequently appear on company balance sheets, and our company has both kinds. The first type listed is *EARNED* surplus (Item 27). Earned surplus is roughly similar to your own savings. To the corporation, earned surplus is that part of net income which has not been paid to stockholders as dividends. It still belongs to you, but the directors have decided that it is best for the company and the stockholders to keep it in the business. The surplus may be invested in the plant just as you might invest part of your savings in your home. It may also be in cash or securities.

In addition to the earned surplus, our company also has a *CAPITAL* surplus (Item 28) of $1,900.00, which the balance sheet explains arose from selling the stock at a higher cost per share than is given as its stated value. A little arithmetic shows that the stock is carried on the books at $2.50 a share while the capital surplus amounts to $4.75 a share. From this we know that the company actually received an average of $7.25 net a share for the stock when it was sold.

WHAT DOES THE BALANCE SHEET SHOW?

Before we undertake to analyze the balance sheet figures, a word on just what an investor can expect to learn is in order. A generation or more ago, before present accounting standards had gained wide acceptance, considerable imagination went into the preparation of balance sheets. This, naturally, made the public skeptical of financial reports. Today, there is no substantial ground for skepticism. The certified public accountant, the listing requirements of the national stock exchanges, and the regulations of the Securities and Exchange Commission have, for all practical purposes, removed the grounds for doubting the good faith of financial reports.

The investor, however, is still faced with the task of determining the significance of the figures. As we have already seen, a number of items are based, to a large degree, upon estimates, while others are, of necessity, somewhat arbitrary.

NET WORKING CAPITAL

There is one very important thing that we can find from the balance sheet and accept with the full confidence that we know what we are dealing with. That is net working capital, sometimes simply called working capital.

On the asset side of our balance sheet, we have added up all of the current assets and show the total as Item 6. On the liability side, Item 20 gives the total of current liabilities. *Net working capital* or *net current assets* is the difference left after subtracting current liabilities from current assets. If you consider yourself an investor rather than a speculator, you should always insist that any company in which you invest have a comfortable amount of working capital. The ability of a company to meet its obligations with ease, expand its volume as business expands and take advantage of opportunities as they present themselves, is, to an important degree, determined by its working capital.

Probably the question in your mind is: "*Just what does 'comfortable amount*' of working capital mean?" Well, there are several methods used by analysts to judge whether a particular company has a sound working capital position. The first rough test for an industrial company is to compare the working capital figure with the current liability total. Most analysts say that minimum safety requires that net working capital at least equal current liabilities. Or, put another way, current assets should be at least twice as large as current liabilities.

There are so many different kinds of companies, however, that this test requires a great deal of modification if it is to be really helpful in analyzing companies in different industries. To help you interpret the current position of a company in which you are considering investing, the *current ratio* is more helpful than the dollar total of working capital. The current ratio is current assets divided by current liabilities.

In addition to working capital and current ratio, there are two other ways of testing the adequacy of the current position. *Net quick assets* provide a rigorous and important test of a company's ability to meet its current obligations. Net quick assets are found by taking total current assets (Item 6) and subtracting the value of inventories (Item 5). A well-fixed industrial company should show a reasonable excess of quick assets over current liabilities.

Finally, many analysts say that a good industrial company should have at least as much working capital (current assets less current liabilities) as the total book value of its bonds and preferred stock. In other words, current liabilities, bonded debt, and preferred stock *altogether* should not exceed the current assets.

INVENTORY AND INVENTORY TURNOVER

In the recent past, there has been much talk of inventories. Many commentators have said that these carry a serious danger to company earnings if management allows them to increase too much. Of course, this has always been true, but present high prices have made everyone more inventory-conscious than usual.

There are several dangers in a large inventory position. In the first place, sharp drop in price may cause serious losses; also, a large inventory may indicate that the company has accumulated a big supply of unsalable merchandise. The question still remains, however: "What do we mean by large inventory?"

As you certainly realize, an inventory is large or small only in terms of the yearly turnover and the type of business. We can discover the annual turnover of our sample company by dividing inventories (Item 5) into total annual sales (item "a" on the income account).

It is also interesting to compare the value of the inventory of a company being studied with total current assets. Again, however, there is considerable variation between different types of companies, so that the relationship becomes significant only when compared with similar companies.

NET BOOK VALUE OF SECURITIES

There is one other very important thing that can be gotten from the balance sheet, and that is the net book or equity value of the company's securities. We can calculate the net book value of each of the three types of securities our company has outstanding by a little very simple arithmetic. *Book value* means *the value at which something is carried on the books of the company.*

The full rights of the bondholders come before any of the rights of the stockholders, so, to find the net book value or net tangible assets backing up the bonds we add together the balance sheet value of the bonds, preferred stock, common stock, reserve, and surplus. This gives us a total of $9,630,000, (We would not include contingency reserve if we were reasonably sure the contingency was going to arise, but, as general reserves are often equivalent to surplus, it is, usually, best to treat the reserve just as though it were surplus.) However, part of this value represents the goodwill and patents carried at $100,000, which is not a tangible item, so, to be conservative, we subtract this amount, leaving $9,530,000 as the total net book value of the bonds. This is equivalent to $4,765 for each $1,000 bond, a generous figure. To calculate the net book value of the preferred stock, we must eliminate the face value of the bonds, and then, following the same procedure, add the value of the preferred stock, common stock, reserve, and surplus, and subtract goodwill. This gives us a total net book value for the preferred stock of $7,530 or $753 for each share of $100 par value preferred. This is also very good coverage for the preferred stock, but we must examine current earnings before becoming too enthusiastic about the value of any security.

The net book value of the common stock, while an interesting figure, is not so important as the coverage on the senior securities. In case of liquidation, there is seldom much left for the common stockholders because of the normal loss in value of company assets when they are put up for sale, as mentioned before. The book value figure, however, does give us a basis for comparison with other companies. Comparisons of net book value over a period of years also show us if the company is a soundly growing one or, on the other hand, is losing ground. Earnings, however, are our important measure of common stock values, as we will see shortly.

The net book value of the common stock is found by adding the stated value of the common stock, reserves, and surplus and then subtracting patents and goodwill. This gives us a total net book value of $6,530,000. As there are 400,000 shares of common outstanding, each share has a net book value of $16.32. You must be careful not to be misled by book value figures, particularly of common stock. Profitable companies (Coca-Cola, for example) often show a very low net book value and very substantial earnings. Railroads, on the other hand, may show a high book value for their common stock but have such low or irregular earnings that the market price of the stock is much less than its apparent book value. Banks, insurance companies, and investment trusts are exceptions to what we have said about common stock net book value. As their assets are largely liquid (i.e., cash, accounts receivable, and marketable securities), the book value of their common stock sometimes indicates its value very accurately.

PROPORTION OF BONDS, PREFERRED AND COMMON STOCK

Before investing, you will want to know the proportion of each kind of security issued by the company you are considering. A high proportion of bonds reduces the attractiveness of both the preferred and common stock, while too large an amount of preferred detracts from the value of the common.

The *bond ratio* is found by dividing the face value of the bonds (Item 21), or $2,000,000, by the total value of the bonds, preferred stock, common stock, reserve, and surplus, or $9,630,000. This shows that bonds amount to about 20 percent of the total of bonds, capital, and surplus.

The *preferred stock ratio* is found in the same way, only we divide the stated value of the preferred stock by the total of the other five items. Since we have half as much preferred stock as we have bonds, the preferred ratio is roughly 10.

Naturally, the *common stock ratio* will be the difference between 100 percent and the totals of the bonds and preferred, or 70 percent in our sample company. You will want to remember that the most valuable method of determining the common stock ratio is in combination with reserve and surplus. The surplus, as we have noted, is additional backing for the common stock and usually represents either original funds paid in to the company in excess of the stated value of the common stock (capital surplus), or undistributed earnings (earned surplus).

Most investment analysts carefully examine industrial companies that have more than about a quarter of their capitalization represented by bonds, while common stock should total at least as much as all senior securities (bonds and preferred issues). When this is not the case, companies often find it difficult to raise new capital. Banks don't like to lend them money because of the already large debt, and it is sometimes difficult to sell common stock because of all the bond interest or preferred dividends that must be paid before anything is available for the common stockholder.

Railroads and public utility companies are exceptions to most of the rules of thumb that we use in discussing The ABC Manufacturing Company, Inc. Their situation is different because of the tremendous amounts of money they have invested in their fixed assets, their small inventories and he ease with which they can collect their receivables. Senior securities of railroads and utility companies frequently amount to more than half of their capitalization, Speculators often interest themselves in companies that have a high proportion of debt or preferred stock because of the *leverage factor.* A simple illustration will show why. Let us take, for example, a company with $10,000,000 of 4 percent bonds outstanding. If the company is earning $440,000 before bond interest, there will be only $40,000 left for the common stock ($10,000,000 at 4% equals $400,000). However, an increase of only 10 percent in earnings (to $484,000) will leave $84,000 for common stock dividends, or an increase of more than 100 percent. If there is only a small common issue, the increase in earnings per share would appear very impressive.

You have probably already noticed that a decline of 10 percent in earnings would not only wipe out everything available for the common stock, but result in the company being unable to cover its full interest on its bonds without dipping into surplus. This is the great danger of so-called high leverage stocks and also illustrates the fundamental weakness of companies that have a disproportionate amount of debt or preferred stock. Investors would do well to steer clear of them. Speculators, however, will continue to be fascinated by the market opportunities they offer.

THE INCOME ACCOUNT

The fundamental soundness of a company, as shown by its balance sheet, is important to investors, but of even greater interest is the record of its operation. Its financial structure shows much of its ability to weather storms and pick up speed when times are good. It is the income record, however, that shows us how a company is actually doing and gives us our best guide to the future.

The *Consolidated Income and Earned Surplus* account of our company is stated on the next page. Follow the items given there and we will find out just how our company earned its money, what it did with its earnings, and what it all means in terms of our three classes of securities. We have used a combined income and surplus account because it is the form most frequently followed by industrial companies. However, sometimes the two statements are given separately. Also, a variety of names are used to describe this same part of the financial report. Sometimes it is called profit and loss account, sometimes *record of earnings*, and, often, simply *income account*. They are all the same thing.

The details that you will find on different income statements also vary a great deal. Some companies show only eight or ten separate items, while others will give a page or more of closely spaced entries that break down each individual type of revenue or cost. We have tried to strike a balance between extremes; give the major items that are in most income statements, omitting details that are only interesting to the expert analyst.

The most important source of revenue always makes up the first item on the income statement. In our company, it is *Net Sales* (Item "a"). If it were a railroad or a utility instead of a manufacturer, this item would be called *gross revenues.* In any case, it represents the money paid into the company by its customers. Net sales are given to show that the figure represents the amount of money actually received after allowing for discounts and returned goods.

Net sales or gross revenues, you will note, is given before any kind of miscellaneous revenue that might have been received from investments, the sale of company property, tax refunds, or the like. A well-prepared income statement is always set up this way so that the stockholder can estimate the success of the company in fulfilling its major job of selling goods or service. If this were not so, you could not tell whether the company was really losing or making money on its operations, particularly over the last few years when tax rebates and other unusual things have often had great influence on final net income figures.

The ABC Manufacturing Company, Inc.
CONSOLIDATED INCOME AND EARNED SURPLUS
For the Year Ended December 31

Item		
a. Sales		$10,000,000
b. COST OF SALES, EXPENSES AND OTHER OPERATING CHARGES:		
c. Cost of Goods Sold	$7,000,000	
d. Selling, Administrative & Gen. Expenses	500,000	
e. Depreciation	200,000	
f. Maintenance and Repairs	400,000	
g. Taxes (Other than Federal Inc. Taxes)	300,000	
h. NET PROFIT FROM OPERATIONS		8,400,000
i. OTHER INCOME:		$1,600,000
j. Royalties and Dividends	$250,000	
k. Interest	25,000	
l. TOTAL		$1,875,000
m. INTEREST CHARGES:		
n. Interest on Funded Debt	$70,000	
o. Other Interest	20,000	90,000
p. NET INCOME BEFORE PROVISION FOR FED. INCOME TAXES		$1,785,000
q. PROVISION FOR FEDERAL INCOME TAXES		678,300
r. NET INCOME		$1,106,700
s. DIVIDENDS		
t. Preferred Stock - $5.00 Per Share	$50,000	
u. Common Stock - $1.00 Per Share	400,000	
v. PROVISION FOR CONTINGENCIES	200,000	650,000
w. BALANCE CARRIED TO EARNED SURPLUS		456,700
x, EARNED SURPLUS – JANUARY 1		3,073,000
y. EARNED SURPLUS – DECEMBER 31		$3,530,000

COST OF SALES

A general heading, *Cost of Sales, Expenses, and Other Operating Charges* (Item "b") is characteristic of a manufacturing company, but a utility company or railroad would call all of these things *operating expenses*.

The most important subdivision is *Cost of Goods Sold* (Item "c"). Included under cost of goods sold are all of the expenses that go directly into the manufacture of the products the company sells—raw materials, wages, freight, power, and rent. We have lumped these expenses together, as many companies do. Sometimes, however, you will find each item listed separately. Analyzing a detailed income account is a pretty technical operation and had best be left to the expert.

We have shown separately, opposite "d," the *Selling, Administrative and General Expenses* of the past year. Unfortunately, there is little uniformity among companies in their treatment of these important non-manufacturing costs. Our figure includes the expenses of management; that is, executive salaries and clerical costs; commissions and salaries paid to salesmen; advertising expenses, and the like.

Depreciation ("e") shows us the amount that the company transferred from income during the year to the depreciation reserve that we ran across before as Item "11" on the balance sheet (Page 2). Depreciation must be charged against income unless the company is going to live on its own fat, something that no company can do for long and stay out of bankruptcy.

MAINTENANCE

Maintenance and Repairs (Item "f") represents the money spent to keep the plant in good operating order. For example, the truck that we mentioned under depreciation must be kept running day by day. The cost of new tires, recharging the battery, painting and mechanical repairs are all maintenance costs. Despite this day-to-day work on the truck, the company must still provide for the time when it wears out—hence, the reserve for depreciation.

You can readily understand from your own experience the close connection between maintenance and depreciation. If you do not take good care of your own car, you will have to buy a new one sooner than you would had you maintained it well. Corporations face the same problem with all of their equipment. If they do not do a good job of maintenance, much more will have to be set aside for depreciation to replace the abused tools and property.

Taxes are always with us. A profitable company always pays at least two types of taxes. One group of taxes are paid without regard to profits, and include real estate taxes, excise taxes, social security, and the like (Item "g"). As these payments are a direct part of the cost of doing business, they must be included before we can determine the *Net Profit From Operations* (Item "h").

Net Profit From Operations (sometimes called *gross profit*) tells us what the company made from manufacturing and selling its products. It is an interesting figure to investors because it indicates how efficiently and successfully the company operates in its primary purpose as a creator of wealth. As a glance at the income account will tell you, there are still several other items to be deducted before the stockholder can hope to get anything. You can also easily imagine that for many companies these other items may spell the difference between profit and loss. For these reasons, we use net profit from operations as an indicator of progress in manufacturing and merchandising efficiency, not as a judge of the investment quality of securities.

Miscellaneous Income not connected with the major purpose of the company is generally listed after net profit from operations. There are quite a number of ways that corporations increase their income, including interest and dividends on securities they own, fees for special services performed, royalties on patents they allow others to use, and tax refunds. Our income statement shows *Other Income* as Item "i," under which is shown income from *Royalties* and *Dividends* (Item "j"), and as a separate entry, *Interest* (Item "k") which the company received from its bond investments. The *Total* of other income (Item "l") shows us how much The ABC Manufacturing Company received from so-called *outside activities*. Corporations with diversified interests often receive tremendous amounts of other income.

INTEREST CHARGES

There is one other class of expenses that must be deducted from our income before we can determine the base on which taxes are paid, and that is *Interest Charges* (Item "m"). As our company has $2,000,000 worth of 3 ½ percent bonds outstanding, it will pay *Interest* on Funded Debt of $70,000 (Item "n"). During the year, the company also borrowed money from the bank, on which it, of course, paid interest, shown as *Other Interest* (Item "o").

Net Income Before Provision for Federal Income Taxes ("Item "p") is an interesting figure for historical comparison. It shows us how profitable the company was in all of its various operations. A comparison of this entry over a period of years will enable you to see how well the company had been doing as a business institution before the government stepped in for its share of net earnings. Federal taxes have varied so much in recent years that earnings before taxes are often a real help in judging business progress.

A few paragraphs back we mentioned that a profitable corporation pays two general types of taxes. We have already discussed those that are paid without reference to profits. *Provision for Federal Income Taxes* (Item "q") is ordinarily figured on the total income of the company after normal business expenses, and so appears on our income account below these charges. Bond interest, for example, as it is payment on a loan, is deducted beforehand. Preferred and common stock dividends, which are profits that go to owners of the company, come after all charges and taxes.

NET INCOME

After we have deducted all of our expenses and income taxes from total income, we get *Net Income* (Item "r"). Net income is the most interesting figure of all to the investor. Net income is the amount available to pay dividends on the preferred and common stock. From the balance sheet, we have learned a good deal about the company's stability and soundness of structure; from net profit from operations, we judge whether the company is improving in industrial efficiency. Net income tells us whether the securities of the company are likely to be a profitable investment.

The figure given for a single year is not nearly all of the store, however. As we have noted before, the historical record is usually more important than the figure for any given year. This is just as true of net income as any other item. So many things change from year to year that care must be taken not to draw hasty conclusions. During the war, Excess Profits Taxes had a tremendous effect on the earnings of many companies. In the next few years, carryback tax credits allowed some companies to show a net profit despite the fact that they had operated at a loss. Even net income can be a misleading figure unless one examines it carefully. A rough and easy way of judging how sound a figure it is would be to compare it with previous years.

The investor in stocks has a vital interest in *Dividends* (Item "s"). The first dividend that our company must pay is that on its *Preferred Stock* (Item "t"). Some companies will even pay preferred dividends out of earned surplus accumulated in the past if the net income is not large enough, but such a company is skating on thin ice unless the situation is most unusual.

The directors of our company decided to pay dividends totaling ($400,000 on the *Common Stock*, or $1 a share (Item "u"). As we have noted before, the amount of dividends paid is not determined by net income, but by a decision of the stockholders' representatives–the company's directors. Common dividends, just like preferred dividends, can be paid out of surplus if there is little or no net income. Sometimes companies do this if they have a long history of regular payments and don't want to spoil the record because of some special temporary situation that caused them to lose money. This occurs even less frequently and is more dangerous than paying preferred dividends out of surplus.

It is much more common, on the contrary, to plough earnings back into the business–a phrase you frequently see on the financial pages and in company reports. The directors of our typical company have decided to pay only $1 on the common stock, though net income would have permitted them to pay much more. They decided that the company should save the difference.

The next entry on our income account, *Provision for Contingencies* (Item "v") shows us where our reserve for contingencies arose. The treasurer of our typical company has put the provision for contingencies after dividends. However, you will discover, if you look at very many financial reports, that it is sometimes placed above net income.

All of the net income that was not paid out as dividends, or set aside for contingencies, is shown as *Balance Carried to Earned Surplus* (Item "w"). In other words, it is kept in the business. In previous years, the company had also earned more than it paid out so it had already accumulated by the beginning of the year an earned surplus of $3,073,000 (Item "x"). When we total the earned surplus accumulated during the year to that which the company had at the first of the year, we get the total earned surplus at the end of the year (Item "y"). You will notice that the total here is the same as that which we ran across on the balance sheet as Item 27.

Not all companies combine their income and surplus account. When they do not, you will find that *balance carried to surplus* will be the last item on the income account. The statement of consolidated surplus would appear as a third section of the corporation's financial report. A separate surplus account might be used if the company shifted funds for reserves to surplus during the year or made any other major changes in its method of treating the surplus account.

ANALYZING THE INCOME ACCOUNT

The income account, like the balance sheet, will tell us a lot more if we make a few detailed comparisons. The size of the totals on an income account doesn't mean much by itself. A company can have hundreds of millions of dollars in net sales and be a very bad investment. On the other hand, even a very modest profit in round figure may make a security attractive if there are only a small number of shares outstanding.

Before you select a company for investment, you will want to know something of its *margin of profit*, and how this figure has changed over the years. Finding the margin of profit is very simple. We just divide the net profit from operations (Item "h") by net sales (Item "a"). The figure we get (0.16) shows us that the company made a profit of 16 percent from operations. By itself, though, this is not very helpful. We can make it significant in two ways.

In the first place, we can compare it with the margin of profit in previous years, and, from this comparison, learn if the company excels other companies that do a similar type of business. If the margin of profit of our company is very low in comparison with other companies in the same field, it is an unhealthy sign. Naturally, if it is high, we have grounds to be optimistic.

Analysts also frequently use *operating ratio* for the same purpose. The operating ratio is the complement of the margin of profit. The margin of profit of our typical company is 16. The operating ratio is 84. You can find the operating ratio either by subtracting the margin of profit from 100 or dividing the total of operating costs ($8,400,000) by net sales ($10,000,000).

The margin of profit figure and the operating ratio, like all of those ratios we examined in connection with the balance sheet, give us general information about the company, help us judge its prospects for the future. All of these comparisons have significance for the long term as they tell us about the fundamental economic condition of the company. But you still have the right to ask: "Are the securities good investments for me now?"

Investors, as opposed to speculators, are primarily interested in two things. The first is safety for their capital and the second, regularity of income. They are also interested in the rate of return on their investment but, as you will see, the rate of return will be affected by the importance placed on safety and regularity. High income implies risk. Safety must be bought by accepting a lower return.

The safety of any security is determined primarily by the earnings of the company that are available to pay interest or dividends on the particular issues. Again, though, round dollar figures aren't of much help to us. What we want to know is the relationship between the total money available and the requirements for each of the securities issued by the company.

INTEREST COVERAGE

As the bonds of our company represent part of its debt, the first thing we want to know is how easily the company can pay the interest. From the income account we see that the company had total income of $1,875,000 (Item "1"). The interest charge on our bonds each year is $70,000 (3½ percent of $2,000,000–Item 21 on the balance sheet). Dividing total income by bond interest charges ($1,875,000 by $70,000) shows us that the company earned its bond interest 26 times over. Even after income taxes, bond interest was earned 17 times, a method of testing employed by conservative analysts. Before an industrial bond should be considered a safe investment, so our company has a wide margin of safety.

To calculate the *preferred dividend coverage* (i.e., the number of times preferred dividends were earned), we must use net income as our base, as Federal Income Taxes and all interest charges must be paid before anything is available for stockholders. As we have 10,000 shares of $100 par value of preferred stock which pays a dividend of 5 percent, the total dividend requirement for the preferred stock is $50,000 (Items 24 on the balance sheet and "t" on the income account).

EARNINGS PER COMMON SHARE

The buyer of common stocks is often more concerned with the earnings per share of his stock than he is with the dividend. It is usually earnings per share or, rather, prospective earnings per share, that influence stock market prices. Our income account does not show the earnings available for the common stock, so we must calculate it ourselves. It is net income less preferred dividends (Items "r"- "t"), or $1,056,700. From the balance sheet, we know that there are 400,000 shares outstanding, so the company earned about $2.64 per share.

All of these ratios have been calculated for a single year. It cannot be emphasized too strongly, however, that the record is more important to the investor than the report of any single year. By all the tests we have employed, both the bonds and the preferred stock of our typical company appear to be very good investments, if their market prices were not too high. The investor would want to look back, however, to determine whether the operations were reasonably typical of the company.

Bonds and preferred stocks that are very safe usually sell at pretty high prices, so the yield to the investor is small. For example, if our company has been showing about the same coverage on its preferred dividends for many years and there is good reason to believe that the future will be equally kind, the company would probably replace the old 5 percent preferred with a new issue paying a lower rate, perhaps 4 percent.

STOCK PRICES

As the common stock does not receive a guaranteed dividend, its market value is determined by a great variety of influences in addition to the present yield of the stock measured by its dividends. The stock market, by bringing together buyers and sellers from all over the world, reflects their composite judgment of the present and future value of the stock. We cannot attempt here to write a treatise on the stock market. There is one important ratio, however, that every common stock buyer considers. That is the ratio of earnings to market price.

The so-called *price-earnings ratio* is simply the earnings per share on the common stock divided into the market price. Our typical company earned $2.64 a common share in the year. If the stock were selling at $30 a share, its price-earnings ratio would be about 11.4. This is the basis figure that you would want to use in comparing the common stock of this particular company with other similar stocks.

17

IMPORTANT TERMS AND CONCEPTS

<u>LIABILITIES</u>

WHAT THE COMPANY OWES—+ RESERVES + SURPLUS + STOCKHOLDERS INTEREST IN THE COMPANY

<u>ASSETS</u>

WHAT THE COMPANY OWNS– + WHAT IS OWED TO THE COMPANY

<u>FIXED ASSETS</u>

MACHINERY, EQUIPMENT, BUILDINGS, ETC.

<u>EXAMPLES OF FIXED ASSETS</u>

DESKS, TABLES, FILING CABINETS, BUILDINGS, LAND, TIMBERLAND, CARS AND TRUCKS, LOCOMOTIVES AND FREIGHT CARS, SHIPYARDS, OIL LANDS, ORE DEPOSITS, FOUNDRIES

<u>EXAMPLES OF:</u>

<u>PREPAID EXPENSES</u>

PREPAID INSURANCE, PREPAID RENT, PREPAIDD ROYALTIES AND PREPAID INTEREST

<u>DEFERRED CHARGES</u>

AMORTIZATION OF BOND DISCOUNT, ORGANIZATION EXPENSE, MOVING EXPENSES, DEVELOPMENT EXPENSES

<u>ACCOUNTS PAYABLE</u>

BILLS THE COMPANY OWES TO OTHERS

<u>BONDHOLDERS ARE CREDITORS</u>

BOND CERTIFICATES ARE IOU'S ISSUED BY A COMPANY BACKED BY A PLEDGE

<u>BONDHOLDERS ARE OWNERS</u>

A STOCK CERTIFICATE IS EVIDENCE OF THE SHAREHOLDER'S OWNERSHIP

<u>EARNED SURPLUS</u>

INCOME PLOWED BACK INTO THE BUSINESS

<u>NET SALES</u>

GROSS SALES MINUS DISCOUNTS AND RETURNED GOODS

<u>NET INCOME</u>

= TOTAL INCOME MINUS ALL EXPENSES AND INCOME TAXES

www.ingramcontent.com/pod-product-compliance
Lightning Source LLC
Chambersburg PA
CBHW081821300426
44116CB00014B/2442
* 9 7 8 1 7 9 9 3 0 9 9 2 5 *